WHAT'S THE POINT OF BEING GREEN?

HELP!

With thanks to consultant
Richard Cornes
Climatic Research Unit
University of East Anglia

Designed by Matthew Lilly

Illustrated by Jan McCafferty

Created for Franklin Watts by
two's COMPANY

First published in 2010 by Franklin Watts
338 Euston Road, London NW1 3BH

Franklin Watts Australia
Level 17/207 Kent Street, Sydney, NSW 2000

Franklin Watts is a division of Hachette
Children's Books, an Hachette UK company.
www.hachette.co.uk

A CIP catalogue record for this book
is available from the British Library.

Dewey number: 333.7'2

ISBN: 978 0 7496 9316 9

Printed in China.

WHAT'S THE POINT OF BEING GREEN?

JACQUI BAILEY

The world is changing, and we have to change too!

W
FRANKLIN WATTS
LONDON·SYDNEY

Are you ready?

CONTENTS

It's all here!

SO, WHAT'S THE PROBLEM?

Well, let's start with a story...

Imagine you are sitting on a big, comfy life raft. Maybe you are reading a book, or listening to your iPod.

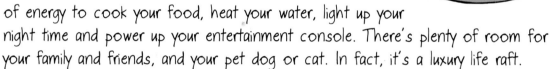

The life raft has everything you need. It supplies you with food and water, a shelter that keeps you warm when it's cold or cool when it's hot, and a source of energy to cook your food, heat your water, light up your night time and power up your entertainment console. There's plenty of room for your family and friends, and your pet dog or cat. In fact, it's a luxury life raft.

Of course, it's not really going anywhere, but that's okay because there isn't anywhere to go. It is floating on an endless ocean. There are no islands or continents to go to, not even any other life rafts. Yours is the only one.

The thing is, your life raft has sprung a few leaks and you've been so busy doing other things you haven't noticed. But now it is not working so well, and bits of it are starting to fall off. It has to be fixed, otherwise it will stop providing everything you need. It could even sink, and then where would you be?

You can't tow it to a garage or a boat shed, or get someone in to fix it. YOU have to fix it. You and your family and your friends — and even your pet dog or cat. Because it's your life raft, and it's the only one there is.

BACK TO EARTH

Okay, so that story is a bit simplistic, but you get the idea. Our planet is not just 'good old Earth, always been here, always will be here', it is our life raft – and, as far as we know, it is unique in the universe. In other words, it is the only one there is.

But just like the life raft in the story, our planet is no longer working so well and it needs fixing, otherwise it too will stop providing us with all the things we need. And the only people who can fix it are us – all of us.

CHANGING TIMES

Why isn't it working? Well, the short answer is that our **climate** is changing – overall, the world is getting hotter. Okay, you might think. That doesn't sound so

Are you ready to fix the planet?

FACT!

Until recently many people argued over whether or not **global warming** was happening, and if it was, what had caused it. Now most scientists agree that it really is happening and that a lot of the changes they have recorded over the past 50 years have happened **because of us.**

You've got to face the facts. IT'S HAPPENING!

bad. Maybe we'll have warmer summers, or even warmer winters.

But actually, it is bad. Because although climates generally differ from place to place around the world, when the average temperature of the world changes by even a few degrees, things happen – to the weather, to the land and the oceans, and to the plants and animals that live on the land and in the oceans – including us.

Why are these things happening, and what can we do about it? Well, that is what this book is about, but before we get into the details we should start by looking backwards.

Let's go back in time...

A QUICK BIT OF HISTORY

One of the reasons why we know that global climate change can have a disastrous effect on the planet is because it has happened before – more than once.

The Earth has a long history – more than 4 billion years long (that's four thousand million years) – although to be honest, as far as life is concerned, not a lot happened for the first few billion. Things only really got interesting when the first animals appeared, about 600 million years ago. Okay, so they were mainly sponges and jellyfish, but then came lots of weird-looking sea creatures, and then fish, land plants and insects, and then all kinds of amphibians and reptiles.

Then there was a dramatic change in the Earth's climate – and almost all the plant and animal species in the world disappeared!

WIPED OUT!

If it can happen to us dinosaurs...

Scientists call this a **mass extinction**, and it happened about 250 million years ago. It wasn't the first mass extinction, there were at least two others before this one, but it was by far the biggest. It took more than 20 million years for the Earth to recover. Millions of species had vanished forever but new ones gradually appeared. Among them, the first tiny mammals and the first dinosaurs.

...it can happen to you!

Then about 200 million years ago there was another mass extinction. This time about half of the world's species died out, and the dinosaurs took over the Earth.

And then it happened again. About 65 million years ago there was another dramatic change and another mass extinction. Three-quarters of the world's plant and animal species were wiped out – and all of the dinosaurs went with them.

WHY DO EXTINCTIONS HAPPEN?

These mass extinctions were all so long ago, it's hard to know exactly what made them happen.

Some, at least, may have been set off by massive collisions between the Earth and meteors, or by huge volcanic eruptions. But, even though events such as these would cause an enormous amount of destruction, it is unlikely that they alone could be responsible for the huge loss of life that occurred.

When **volcanoes erupt** they throw out vast clouds of dust and ash, blocking the warmth and energy of the Sun from the Earth.

However, they could have started a chain of events that led to big changes in the world's climate and this would have had a devastating effect on life.

Now many scientists think the world is on the brink of another mass extinction – but this time, unlike all of the others, the chain of events has been **started by US**.

How do we know that?

We know about mass extinctions because of the clues they leave behind, buried in the Earth's rocks. **Palaeontologists** are people who study the remains of animals and plants that existed in prehistoric times. They look at the different layers of rocks laid down over millions of years and sift through them, searching for any fossils they may contain. From these fossils the palaeontologists are able to work out how old the rocks are and what types of life forms existed when the rocks were formed.

FACT!

In 2008, the Red List, published by the International Union for Conservation of Nature and Natural Resources (IUCN), showed that nearly one quarter of the world's mammal species are currently under threat of extinction.

ECO-TIP... Protect wildlife – don't buy souvenir seashells or corals.

In the last ice age, vast ice sheets covered much of North America, northern Europe and the far north of Asia.

GETTING COLDER

Mass extinctions don't happen very often – tens of millions of years roll by between them – but smaller changes in the global climate are happening all the time. Over thousands of years, the world can get warmer or colder.

These slow shifts in global temperature take place because of regular, long-term changes in the way the Earth **orbits** the Sun. The shift in temperature may be only a few degrees, but the effect can be big. Around 18,000 years ago, for example, the average world temperature was only 5°C colder than it is now and a large part of the planet was covered in ice.

Eventually the world warmed up a bit and the ice sheets shrank. For the past 10,000 years, Earth's climate has been more or less stable – at least, it has until now.

GETTING WARMER

Over the last 100 years, the global temperature has begun climbing, far more quickly than before. As the world gets warmer the remaining glaciers and land ice will melt. Oceans will warm up and sea levels will rise, swamping coasts and river inlets.

The weather will get weirder in some areas, with more storms, hurricanes and floods, or with more droughts. Long-term changes in the weather will affect habitats, making it harder for plants and animals to survive, including humans. We will start to run out of food, fresh water, and space to live.

Because of **global warming**, storms and floods will happen more often and with more impact.

It is hard to know precisely how quickly the climate is changing, but it is generally accepted that from 1906–2005, surface temperature worldwide increased by almost 1°C.

Scientists now fear that in the next 100 years temperatures could rocket to as much as 6°C above present levels, and they say that the longer we take to do anything about it the worse it will get. In the past this level of change would have taken thousands of years not hundreds, giving many plant and animal species time to adapt – but at this rate they will not have time, and the effect is likely to be devastating.

Phew!

FACT!

In their 2007 report, the Intergovernmental Panel on Climate Change (IPCC) said that average global temperatures for 11 of the past 12 years (from 1995–2006), were the warmest ever recorded.

ECO-TIP... Turn the central heating down – even 1 degree less saves energy.

HELP!

WHAT CAN WE DO?

Bad though it sounds, we can do something about it, as long as we start doing it now, and the whole world gets involved – every one of us, from governments and politicians to you and me.

Scientists say that if we can limit the temperature increase to a **maximum of 2°C** (a rise which they feel is already unavoidable) we may be able to escape the worst effects of climate change – although by no means all of them.

It won't be easy. It will mean altering the way we live and the way we think about our world. In fact, it will mean that we need to be **more green**! What does that mean? Well, it can mean different things to different people, but in a general way it means being aware of the environment and the impact we have on it, and doing our best to live in a way that helps rather than harms our planet.

There's no time to hang around!

Ready to start? Then let's go...

WHAT ARE WE DOING TO THE CLIMATE?

To understand how the Earth's climate is changing, it's useful to know a little bit about how it works.

Global climate is affected by all sorts of things – the amount of energy (heat and light) coming from the Sun (solar radiation), the atmosphere surrounding the Earth, and the ways in which the Sun's energy, the atmosphere, and the Earth's surface act together.

SUN

The Sun sends out solar radiation

Some of the Sun's heat bounces off the atmosphere back into space

Some of the Sun's heat hits the Earth

Some surface heat escapes into space

Some surface heat radiates back to Earth

Surface heat radiates upwards

ATMOSPHERE

Sun's heat warms the Earth

EARTH

HOW THE GREENHOUSE EFFECT WORKS.

Hmmm...I think something is missing.

IT'S ALL IN THE ATMOSPHERE

The only reason we can live on Earth at all is because of its atmosphere. Without it, our planet would be just a dry, lifeless rock spinning in space.

The atmosphere is a mixture of gases, dust and water droplets. These form a barrier around the planet which blocks out most of the Sun's harmful rays, but allows some of its heat and light to pass through.

The Sun's heat warms up the surface of the Earth, which then acts like a gigantic radiator by sending heat back into the atmosphere. Some of this surface heat escapes through the atmosphere into space, and some is held in, warming up the air closest to the surface and adding more warmth to the surface itself.

LIVING IN A GREENHOUSE

This process is known as the **greenhouse effect** – because it works like a greenhouse by holding in heat and smoothing out, or lessening, the extremes of hot and cold that happen between day and night.

ON THE SURFACE

Okay, so we all know that Earth's temperature is not entirely smooth and, from our point of view, varies quite a bit from one part of the world to another. Otherwise we could sunbathe at the North Pole or go ice skating on the Amazon.

Partly this is because the Earth is round, which means that the Sun's rays shine directly on the equator but are more spread out in the northern and southern parts of the world. Partly because of seasonal changes. Partly because of the winds that carry heat from one place to another, and partly because of the different ways the land and oceans absorb and release heat.

Like winds, the oceans also make a big difference by moving heat around.

Ocean currents flow around the world carrying hotter or colder water with them and changing the temperature of the air and land nearby.

The land varies in the amount of heat it absorbs and releases, depending on what is covering its surface. Large areas of ice, for example, work like mirrors to reflect most of the Sun's heat back into space, keeping the temperatures low in these parts.

FACT!

The average surface temperature on Earth is 15°C. If it wasn't for the greenhouse effect, it would be –18°C (that's 33°C colder than it is now), which would be like living inside a freezer!

Greenhouse gases

The gases in the atmosphere are mostly nitrogen and oxygen. The rest (about 1 per cent) consists of the gas argon, and minuscule amounts of a group of gases known as **greenhouse gases (GHGs)**. These are carbon dioxide, methane, halocarbons, nitrous oxide and ozone. Together with water vapour, these greenhouse gases are the ONE AND ONLY reason the atmosphere works like a greenhouse.

The amount may be tiny, but the effect is huge!

Oxygen 20.95%

Argon 0.93%

Greenhouse gases 0.04%

Nitrogen 78.08%

ECO-TIP... Don't heat the outside — keep windows and doors shut in winter.

13

I knew it wasn't natural!

GLOBAL WARMING

Most of these GHGs exist naturally in the atmosphere and life on Earth would be a lot more difficult without them, but for more than a century we have been adding to them in ways that are unnatural.

Scientists now think that by increasing the greenhouse gases in the atmosphere we are strengthening their effect, and it is this that is changing the global climate and making the world warmer.

LEADER OF THE PACK

Carbon dioxide (CO2) is usually seen as the biggest baddy of them all because there is more of it than the other GHGs. Carbon dioxide has been in the Earth's atmosphere for almost as long as the Earth itself, and back in the beginning it was a major part of the atmosphere.

Then plants evolved. Plants take in carbon dioxide and use it to make their food, giving out oxygen in the process (it's called **photosynthesis**). Over millions and millions of years,

the plants (especially tiny ocean plants called phytoplankton) removed lots of the carbon dioxide and put oxygen in its place (luckily for us). And because carbon dioxide dissolves in water, some of it is also absorbed by the oceans.

But it is not all one way. Carbon dioxide is put back into the atmosphere when plants and animals die and decay, or are burned. It is also produced as a waste product by plants when they use energy to grow, and when animals breathe out.

CHANGING THE BALANCE

Eventually the levels of CO2 in the atmosphere achieved a balance – until the Industrial Revolution happened and we **added motors to machines**.

Motorised machines radically changed our lives and our world – in many ways for the better (after all, what would we

FACT!

Carbon dioxide can stay in the atmosphere for between 50 to 200 years, continuing to have an effect long after it was produced.

Maybe this will help?

Most fossil fuels are burned inside huge power plants like this one to make electricity, so every time you dry your hair, watch TV, or boil a kettle you are adding **CO_2 emissions** to the atmosphere.

do without the electric toothbrush!). But they also need vast amounts of energy – to build them and make them work. Most of that energy comes from burning **fossil fuels** (coal, oil and natural gas), and burning fossil fuels produces lots of extra carbon dioxide – known as **CO_2 emissions**.

TO MAKE THINGS WORSE

At the same time, we started clearing away forests to make space for more houses, factories and farm land (known as **deforestation**), chopping down millions of trees that would otherwise help to get rid of all that extra CO_2.

On top of that, the trees that are cut down are often burned, which adds more CO_2 to the atmosphere.

In fact, burning vegetation of any sort – whether it is trees, grasslands, or the leftover crop stubble in fields – contributes to CO_2 emissions.

It's building up

Look around you. How much concrete can you see? Bet it's quite a lot. Most roads, bridges, towns and cities in the world are built of concrete. Concrete is made with cement, and manufacturing cement produces huge amounts of CO_2. For every tonne of cement we make we release **one tonne of CO_2**. Currently, about 2 billion tonnes of cement are produced every year, and the figure is still growing, even though some manufacturers are now trying to find ways to reduce their CO_2 output.

OH, NO!
I'm covered in
concrete!

MORE METHANE

So what about the other greenhouse gases? Well, gramme for gramme, **methane** is 21 times more powerful as a greenhouse gas than carbon dioxide! However, it hangs around in the atmosphere for a much shorter time (about 12 years) and, at the moment, there is a lot less of it. Even so, it is on the increase and most of this rise is down to us.

We keep herds of farm cattle, like these, for meat and milk, but they are also major producers of **methane** gas.

Pardon you!

Next time you eat a beefburger think about this. More than one-third of the world's manufactured methane comes from all the cattle and sheep we raise for meat, milk, leather and wool. The methane is made by bacteria helping to break down food in the animals' gut and when their stomachs fill with gas they belch, or fart, it out.

Slurp! Scrunch! Burp!!

BAGS OF GAS

Methane is made when plant or animal matter rots and is broken down by bacteria. It is also produced in the stomachs of animals when they digest food, and it is the main ingredient of the fossil fuel, natural gas.

When we burn natural gas as a fuel it gives off carbon dioxide, but first we have to get it out of the ground and pipe it to where it is needed, and along the way some natural gas leaks directly into the atmosphere.

We add more methane to the atmosphere by spreading fertilizer on our gardens and crops, and in other agricultural processes such as farming rice and livestock. We also produce it by burying our household waste in landfill sites (see page 70).

HANDMADE BY HUMANS

Halocarbons are a group of gases that include CFCs (chlorofluorocarbons), HCFCs (hydrochlorofluorocarbons) and HFCs (hydrofluorocarbons).

Although a few are formed naturally, most of them wouldn't exist at all if we didn't make them. They are used in all sorts of things, from glues, paints and solvents to pesticides and plastics.

CFCs were originally invented as a refrigerator coolant, but were soon being put into all sorts of things — including spray cans.

Phew! Must have been that burger.

There are minuscule amounts of them in the atmosphere, yet their ability to increase global warming is thousands of times greater than CO_2. Also, they are almost indestructible and can last for hundreds of years.

An additional problem is that CFCs also cause damage to the **ozone layer** in the atmosphere. Because of this, many countries now limit the use of CFCs. However, other halocarbons are still being used and are building up in the atmosphere.

NO LAUGHING MATTER

Nitrous oxide is naturally released from the oceans and by bacteria from the soil. It is also manufactured as a pain reliever and an anaesthetic, commonly known as 'laughing gas'.

As with other greenhouse gases it is released by burning fossil fuels and, possibly to a larger extent, by the use of nitrogen fertilizers and in the treatment of our sewage. Nitrous oxide can last more than 100 years in the atmosphere.

Oh, no ozone!

Ozone is made and destroyed naturally by the Sun's rays acting on the oxygen in the atmosphere. Most of it forms high up in the atmosphere in a band known as the ozone layer, where it blocks out most of the harmful ultraviolet (UV) rays from the Sun. CFCs destroy ozone, creating thin areas known as 'holes' in the ozone layer and allowing more UV rays to reach the Earth's surface.

ECO-TIP... Stop and think before you print.

HOW BIG ARE YOUR FEET?

So now you know what greenhouse gases are and what they do to the climate, and maybe you are thinking, 'Okay, but what does this have to do with me? I don't go around chopping down trees, or keeping cattle in my back garden.' And you are right. But you are part of the reason why these things happen – we all are.

Lots of the things we do in our daily lives add GHGs to the atmosphere. What these actions are and how many greenhouse gases they produce can be measured to give what is known as a **carbon footprint**.

A carbon footprint is worked out by adding together the amount of GHGs a person or group is responsible for producing directly (by turning on a TV, for example), with a share of the gases produced in the making or transporting of the products and services they buy.

TRY THIS SIMPLE QUIZ TO SEE HOW BIG YOUR CARBON FEET ARE✱

1 How much time do you spend watching the TV, or dvds?

   a) 3 hours a day or more

   b) 1 hour a day or less

   c) hardly ever

2 When you finish using the TV/computer/games console, do you

   a) turn everything off

   b) leave it on standby

   c) leave everything on — someone else will turn it off

3 How do you travel to school?

   a) by bus or train

   b) by foot or bike

   c) by car

4 What kind of car does your family have?

   a) large saloon or four-wheel drive

   b) medium to small

   c) don't have a car

5 How often do you travel by plane?

   a) almost never

   b) one journey a year (i.e. there and back)

   c) more than one journey a year

✱ If you are reading a library book remember not to mark the book. Then other people can test themselves, too.

6

How often do you buy stuff (clothes, make-up, games, music, dvds, etc.), or ask your parents to get stuff for you?

    a) at least once a week

    b) once a month or less

    c) hardly ever, only when I really need to

7

When you finish drinking something from a bottle or a can do you

    a) bin it

    b) hang onto it until you can recycle it

    c) never drink stuff in cans or bottles

8

When you are brushing your teeth, do you

    a) leave the tap running

    b) just turn on the tap to rinse your brush

    c) don't bother brushing your teeth? *

(* You may be saving on water by not brushing your teeth, but you certainly won't be saving on dental bills, not to mention all that bad breath — ugh!)

How many Earths?

Another way of measuring people's impact on the Earth is by working out their **ecological footprint**. This calculates how much of the Earth's **resources** it takes to support one person (their food, clothing, housing, etc.). On average, we currently need **2 Earths** to support all the people living on the planet. But, not everyone has an equal share of the Earth's resources. If everyone used the same level of resources as people in Canada or the USA, for example, we would need **9 Earths**!

HOW DID YOU DO?

20+
Okay, big foot, you need to get a lot less gassy.

10-20
Not bad, but could do a lot better.

5-10
Well done, either you are very light on your feet, or you live in a remote area with no roads, shops or electricity, but whichever it is you are really helping the planet.

What's your score?

 1 (a) 3 (b) 2 (c) 1
 2 (a) 1 (b) 2 (c) 3
 3 (a) 1 (b) 0 (c) 3
 4 (a) 3 (b) 2 (c) 0
 5 (a) 1 (b) 2 (c) 3
 6 (a) 3 (b) 2 (c) 1
 7 (a) 3 (b) 1 (c) 0
 8 (a) 3 (b) 1 (c) 2

WHY DO WE BURN FOSSIL FUELS?

HOW MANY MACHINES OR GADGETS DO YOU USE IN A DAY?

LET'S IMAGINE YOU GET UP IN THE MORNING AND...

Turn on a light and switch off your radio alarm.

click!

7:25

Go to the bathroom and turn on another light.

click!

Have a hot shower and brush your teeth.

Get dressed and go downstairs (it's winter so the lights are on already).

Have breakfast using milk/butter from the fridge, hot water from a kettle, toast from a toaster, cooked food from an oven or grill.

Stack your used dishes in the dishwasher (instead of leaving them for your mum).

Unplug your mobile phone from its charger, pick up your stuff, head for the street and...

...jump on a bus!

Phew! That's a lot, and your day has barely started. Machines and other devices need energy to make them work, and most of that energy comes from burning fossil fuels – either directly, to heat our buildings, water and food, and power our cars, or indirectly, to make electricity.

BURNING THE PAST

Fossil fuels are found deep under the ground or the oceans. They are formed over millions of years by the weight of layers of rock and sediment pressing down on thick pockets of dead plant and animal matter.

Coal is made from the remains of plants that grew in dank, muddy, swamp forests hundreds of millions of years ago.

Oil and gas are made from the bodies of billions of tiny sea creatures that drifted to the ocean floor and were covered by sediment. Over millions of years they, too, were crushed and heated until they turned into thick, black, liquid oil and then gas.

HOW ARE THEY USED?

A hundred years ago, people burned coal to heat their homes and cook their food, to power steam engines, or in vast furnaces for making metal and other products. Today, most coal is used to make electricity, although it is also used in making cement, glass, paper and other products, and in processing food.

Small amounts of oil naturally seep to the surface of ponds and oceans, and in ancient times it was used for burning in lamps, or even as medicine. In the 1850s, we discovered how to drill deep into the Earth and pump oil up in barrel-loads. Then we found out how to turn it into petrol, diesel, plastics, fabrics, detergents and fertilizers.

Here today, gone tomorrow

Just think, this will all be a pile of coal in a few million years!

Fossil fuels take millions of years to form. Once we have used up all the supplies we can find, whatever is left will be too scarce and too difficult to dig up. Scientists think that if we continue to use fossil fuels at the rate we are now, we could run out of them within the next 100 years.

FACT!

Over 90% of all the coal mined in the USA is used to produce electricity.

Coal is mined in more than 50 countries around the world. Most of it is burned in power stations to make steam. The steam is then used to spin turbine blades to generate electricity.

Gas is often found alongside oil, so when the first oil wells were drilled large deposits of gas were also discovered. At first it was hard to find a use for it, but by the mid-1900s long-distance gas pipelines were built and it became possible to deliver natural gas directly to homes and other buildings for heating, cooking, and for industrial use.

POISONING THE FUTURE

Fossil fuels are a powerful source of energy, but apart from the fact that we will run out of them one day soon, the big problem with burning them is the **pollution** they cause.

Fossil fuels are made from organic materials which means they contain a lot of **carbon**. When carbon is burned it gives off carbon dioxide – as well as other gases such as nitrogen and sulphur, which cause acid rain (see page 60), and mercury pollution, which poisons our water, fish and other wildlife.

Most scientists now agree that CO_2 is the single biggest contributor to the increase of the greenhouse effect and global warming. They say that if we do not cut our CO_2 emissions by at least half in the next 40 years, the worldwide effects of climate change will be disastrous.

Some say that if we really want to limit global warming to no more than 2°C, we need to cut emissions by as much as three-quarters.

Rain washes **mercury pollution** in the air into rivers, lakes and seas, where it can build up and poison the fish we catch and eat.

So who needs electricity?

Dad, where can I plug in my phone?

FACT!

According to the United Nations (see page 85), about 1.7 billion people in Asia and the Pacific still burn fuels such as wood or dried animal dung for their day-to-day energy needs.

WE'VE GOT THE POWER!

One way to cut emissions is to use less energy by using fewer machines. Okay, so we can't just stop using all of our machines, but every one of us can try to use them less, especially when we don't really need to use them.

Electricity is so much a part of our lives that it's hard to imagine living without it. Until you remember that we've been living on the planet for thousands of years and have only used electricity for the last 100 years or so – and some people still barely use it at all. So it should not be too hard to find ways to use it less.

Eating up energy

It is estimated that the amount of energy we currently use worldwide adds **more than 29 billion tonnes** of carbon dioxide to the atmosphere each year. Most of this energy is used by the more economically developed countries, such as the USA, Russia, and Japan. However, many developing countries, especially China and India, are rapidly growing their industries, too – and their energy use. And the more energy they consume, the more CO_2 they produce.

Our atmosphere is in real trouble!

Top 10 producers of CO_2 emissions in 2006

Millions of metric tonnes of carbon dioxide

IRAN	S. KOR	UK	CAN	GER	INDIA	JAPAN	RUSSIA	USA	CHINA
0.47m	0.51m	0.58m	0.61m	0.86m	1.23m	1.25m	1.70m	5.90m	6.02m

ECO-TIP... Every cup of boiled water in your kettle equals 25 cups of CO_2 emissions.

How much food do you **waste**? In the UK alone, about 18 million tonnes of food are thrown away each year. Producing food uses energy so wasting it is wasted energy – and waste dumps filled with rotting food give off methane emissions.

WHAT'S IN YOUR BAG?

And it's not only the energy we use ourselves. Lots of the everyday products we buy are made by machines, wrapped in packaging made by machines, and delivered to shops by machines.

All of which means we can cut our carbon emissions by buying and using fewer, or different products. For example, the whole process of preparing food in a factory, then boxing or wrapping it and transporting it to a supermarket can account for twice as much CO_2 as driving around in a car. Especially if the food has been shipped or flown in from another country.

So…here are a few suggestions for ways you can cut your CO_2 emissions, and you'll find lots more in other parts of this book. (Check out the 'ECO-TIPS' on the sides of the pages, as well.) And, don't forget, the more of us who start saving energy the more carbon we cut, so pass the ideas along to your friends, family, teachers, everyone…

I really should be using a pen and paper to spread the word.

A country the size of Britain could save up to a whole year's worth of energy from one power station if everyone turned off their **standby buttons**.

Switch and save!

Ask your parents to use energy-saving light bulbs wherever possible, and they will not only save energy they will save on their electricity bills as well. (Many old-fashioned styles of lightbulbs have been banned from sale in European countries.)

Be nice to your home – wrap it up. Many older houses and homes leak up to half their heat to the outside world through the walls and roof, let alone the windows. Ask your parents about insulation and if they can do anything to improve it.

Look around the house, how many things have been left on standby? Turn them OFF.

Instead of turning the central heating up when it gets a bit cold outside, put on an extra sweater...cardi...longjohns...slippers – you get the idea. In fact, try turning your hot water and central heating down by one or two degrees. Even one degree less will save energy and money.

Next time you wash your favourite jeans or t-shirt, let it hang around until it's dry instead of putting it in the dryer. Clothes dryers use loads of energy and most of that hot air goes to heat up the outside world.

While we're on the subject of drying – do you really need to use that hairdryer?

Take fewer baths and more showers. Showers use less water and less energy to heat it so you save on two counts.

Next time your parents go food shopping offer to go with them. Find out where the food you buy comes from and try to buy local food where you can, especially fruit and vegetables.

Out with the old – do your parents need a new fridge...toaster...washing machine... something? Get them to check the energy rating before they buy. A-rated appliances are more energy efficient and cheaper to run – better for everyone.

Make sure any packaging on the products you buy is a) necessary, b) recyclable – apples don't taste any better for being boxed and wrapped in plastic.

GETTING INTO ACTION

Of course, try though we might (and we absolutely, definitely should), we won't be able to save the planet all by ourselves – we need help. Lots of help. In fact, we need to bring in the 'heavyweights' – people like the government and other politicians, and the people who run all those big businesses and organisations that make and use so much energy.

If we are going to reduce our carbon emissions by a whacking 50 per cent or more by 2050, all our governments need to take some serious action – fast! Governments can change laws and make new ones – to make sure that people use less energy and use it more efficiently. In fact, some governments are already making changes, but are they doing enough?

The problem is, many governments rely on people to vote them into power, so they tend to avoid doing things they think might make them unpopular. Cutting carbon emissions means telling people and businesses that they have to stop doing things in the way they have been – and not everyone is going to be happy about that.

WRITE ON

If too many of us grumble and groan and refuse to change the way we live, the government will take a lot longer to do anything about it. So for every die-hard energy dinosaur out there, there needs to be twice as many go-for-it greens (or three… or four) telling the government to get on with it.

How do you do that? Well, you could go and stand outside a government building and yell at them! But a much better way is to write to them. Really?

Really!

Dear Prime Minister…

Hmmm! Lots of letters. I think it's time to do something about the planet.

MAIL

What governments can do

- Bring in more regulations to make industries more energy efficient. This means wasting less energy and looking for ways to burn fewer fossil fuels more cleanly.
- Offer more help and financial support to individuals and small businesses to help them cut their emissions at home and at work.
- Invest more money and support in developing alternative, cleaner ways of producing energy.
- Give more help to less economically developed countries to help them develop more efficient, cleaner ways of using energy.

This way please!

PESTER POWER

Write to your Prime Minister, your MP, your local council, the head office of your local supermarket, and anyone else you can think of.

Ask them what they are doing to help cut carbon emissions and why they aren't doing more. Tell them how important you think it is and that you want your country to lead the way and be an example to others.

Get a parent or a teacher to help you. Better still, get together with your friends and classmates and get them to write, too (and your parents, and your teachers). The more the merrier. And don't stop with just one letter – keep on writing. It's called **pester power**. You know how that works – bet you do it to your parents when you really want something. Well, this time put it to good use and…

PESTER FOR THE PLANET!

Right! Now let's take a look at how we can produce energy without burning fossil fuels…

WHAT'S THE ALTERNATIVE?

Fossil fuels may be our biggest sources of energy, but they aren't the only ones. Scientists have known for some time that we will run out of fossil fuels eventually and they have been hunting for alternatives.

One of the difficulties is that we are used to having relatively cheap and efficient energy from coal, oil and gas, and have built up our industries around these fuels. To replace them with cleaner, greener energy sources costs time and money, and so far there has been little pressure to make this change – until now.

GOING NUCLEAR

One, possible solution is **nuclear power**. As well as making bombs and warheads, nuclear power can be used to make electricity. It works by releasing the energy held inside **atoms** – those invisibly small 'bricks' from which everything in the universe is made.

Compared to burning fossil fuels, nuclear energy is efficient and produces almost no greenhouse gases – and what's more, we are already using it.

'Brilliant!' You cry, **'Let's all go nuclear!'**

But (isn't there always a 'but'), there is one major drawback to nuclear power – it produces waste, and that waste is **radioactive** and incredibly poisonous!

FACT!

About 15 per cent of the world's electricity comes from nuclear power, generated by 30 countries around the world, including many European countries, China, Japan and the USA.

Splitting up

To use nuclear power to make electricity, the atoms in a metal called uranium are split apart. This releases a huge amount of heat, which is then used to generate electricity in much the same way as the heat made by burning coal or gas. To start the process, a tiny part of an atom, called a neutron, is fired at one uranium atom. The atom splits and sends out more neutrons to hit other uranium atoms, which split and send out more neutrons, and so on. This is called a chain reaction.

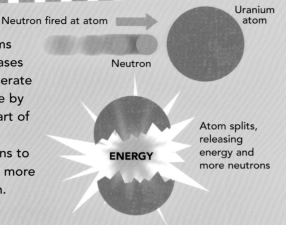

Neutron fired at atom

Neutron

Uranium atom

ENERGY

Atom splits, releasing energy and more neutrons

DEADLY WASTE

Radioactive waste is deadly. Even tiny amounts can kill, and nuclear power plants produce lots of radioactive waste. Anything used in a nuclear power plant that has been contaminated (become radioactive), cannot just be thrown away – it has to be stored, under carefully controlled conditions, for anything from 5 years to 5,000 or more.

Also, there is always the danger that a nuclear power plant could get out of control and accidentally leak radioactive material into the environment. So far, there have been a number of radiation leaks from nuclear power plants, including two major accidents – one at Three Mile Island in the USA in 1979, and the other at Chernobyl in the Ukraine in 1986.

Well, where are we going to bury this lot, then?

Looking for ways to store and dispose of **nuclear waste** is a big problem for the nuclear industry.

Digging it up

Like fossil fuels, uranium is a material that has to be mined out of the ground or the oceans, so although some of it can be recycled and reused, and scientists think we have enough for hundreds of years, eventually it could run out. Plus, at present, uranium is mined by machines that use fossil fuels.

A lump of Uranium ore

YOU DECIDE

Modern nuclear power plants are much safer than they were, and scientists continue to improve them, but the threat of a nuclear accident is always there.

The future of nuclear power is still undecided. Some say it is the only answer to cheap, reliable electricity for all. Others say it is not worth the terrifying possibility of a leak causing lasting damage to the environment. Ultimately, its future rests with the users – that's you and me.

What will your decision be?

EECO-TIP... Turn lights OFF when you don't really need them.

ENDLESS ENERGY

Unlike fossil fuels, or even uranium, there are some sources of energy that will never run out no matter how much we use them. Best of all, they produce no dangerous wastes when they are used. They are **renewable energy sources** and they come from sunlight, water, wind, and the Earth.

HERE COMES THE SUN

The same Sun's energy that warms our planet can also heat our homes and water, cook our food, and even produce electricity. In fact, it can be used in all sorts of ways, although at the moment it is barely used at all.

Buildings can be designed to soak up the Sun's heat and store it so they stay at an even temperature, without needing extra heating for warmth in winter, or air conditioning to cool them down in the summer.

Solar water-heating systems, made of panels of metal or glass tubes, soak up energy from the Sun and use it to heat water. Even in a country like the UK, where it seems like the Sun barely shines, it is possible to heat at least half of an average family's hot water throughout a year.

SUN CELLS

Photovoltaic cells (or solar cells) store sunlight as electricity. You may already have a solar-powered watch or calculator, but bigger versions of solar cells can generate enough electricity to power a factory or a town. Germany, Spain, Japan, and the USA, for example, have all built solar-fuelled power stations in recent years.

Unfortunately **solar power** is not a totally reliable solution – even the sunniest countries sometimes have clouds and rain – but used alongside other renewable energy sources it could come pretty close to solving our energy needs.

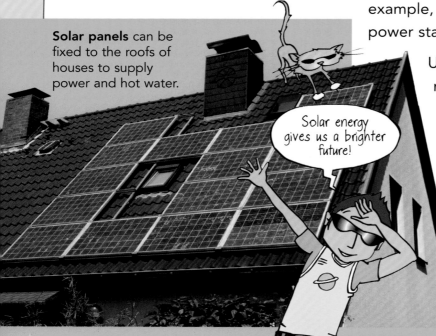

Solar panels can be fixed to the roofs of houses to supply power and hot water.

Solar energy gives us a brighter future!

Sunday lunch

On sunny days, large circular metal dishes, that look like satellite receivers, can be used to focus the Sun's heat to a narrow beam to provide energy for cooking. Even a simple heat box or a curved metal sheet is enough to cook a meal. In countries such as India and Africa, where there is plenty of sunlight but a shortage of fuel or other sources of energy, **solar cookers** are a cheap and efficient alternative.

WHEN WATER FALLS

After nuclear energy, the most widely used alternative to fossil fuels at present is **hydroelectric power**. This uses the energy in moving water to make turbine blades spin around and so generate electricity.

Hydroelectric power plants must be built on a fast-flowing river, which is often dammed to create a lake. This provides a large store of water and allows the water's rate of flow to be controlled. Once the dam is built, hydroelectric power plants provide a clean and fairly reliable source of energy. But although they do not produce pollution or CO_2, there are concerns about other ways in which they can damage the environment.

Hydroelectric power stations are used in a number of countries, especially Canada, Brazil, Norway, Sweden and China.

ON THE DOWN SIDE

For example, when dams are built whole valleys may be flooded, killing many of the plants and animals that lived there and destroying people's homes. Plus, scientists now believe that the drowned and rotting vegetation in the dam water may be adding large amounts of methane to the atmosphere.

ECO-TIP... Save energy by cooking in covered pans.

Turning the tides

Tidal power could be a brilliant alternative to hydroelectricity, without its environmental problems. As tides flow in and out their movement can be made to turn a turbine and generate electricity. Barely used at present, in 2007 one of the world's first turbine tidal energy generators started up in Northern Ireland.

Turbine

Tide direction

Propeller

BLOWING IN THE WIND

If you live in a country with lots of wind rather than fast rivers or coastal water, then **wind power** is an increasingly popular alternative to water power. The blades of these tall, wind-turbine propellers spin around and their movement is used to make electricity.

Collections of wind turbines, known as wind farms, can be built on land or out at sea. In the UK, for example, it is thought that large offshore wind farms could supply enough electricity for every home in the country.

Small wind turbines can also supply power for individual houses and businesses in remote places, and can be used to recharge batteries.

Wind turbines provide a clean and safe source of electricity – as long as the wind blows. They do not seem to harm the environment in any way, although some people complain that the blades can be a danger to birds and bats.

Otherwise, the main argument against them seems to come down to whether you like the look of them or not!

As long as the wind keeps blowing we'll be OK.

The blades of a full-sized **wind turbine** may be up to 40 metres long and can spin around more than 20 times a minute.

UNDERGROUND HEATING

Yet another solution could be to harness the heat of the Earth itself. **Geothermal power** uses either heat from hot springs under the ground, or the heat that builds up in surface soil.

Where hot springs come to the surface, as in Iceland for example, the hot water can be used directly to heat homes or buildings. In other places, wells are drilled deep into the Earth and the steam or hot water is pumped to a power plant to generate electricity.

Half a metre or so underground, average soil temperatures are mostly constant at about 10–15°C. This heat can be soaked up by underground pipes and the warmed water used to heat buildings more efficiently. In summer, the flow can be reversed and warm water sent back to the soil to cool the building down.

The centre of the Earth is hotter than the surface of the Sun. This heat travels outwards from the centre, warming up the layers of rock or water deep underground. In some places, boiling hot water bursts through the surface of the Earth as a hot spring or **geyser**.

FACT!

At present, it is estimated that about 6 per cent of the world's energy comes from nuclear sources, about 6 per cent from hydroelectric sources, and only about **1 per cent** from all other renewable energy sources.

THE BIG QUESTION?

So we know there are other ways of making energy than using fossil fuels, and they are being used – just not enough to make a difference to global warming. People have lots of questions about renewable energy sources, not least the costs involved in building loads of new power plants. But the biggest question, surely, is what will it cost us if we **DON'T** build them?

(Answer: the Earth!)

ECO-TIP... Unplug electronic devices when you are not using them.

BUT WHAT ABOUT CARS?

Yep, you are right. The other major use of fossil fuels – mainly oil – is to power cars and other forms of transport.

Fossil oil is also called **petroleum**, and most of it is turned into petrol, diesel, jet fuel and other machine fuels. Some of these fuels are used for heating, cooking, and industrial processes such as steel-making, but more than half of all the world's petroleum is used for transport.

HONK! HONK!

This is brilliant!

FOSSIL FUELLED

Oil-powered engines were invented by the end of the 1800s, and by the 1920s the first mass-produced cars were hitting the streets. They were a huge success! Today, there are more than 800 million cars and trucks in the world – and most of them are in the more developed countries.

WE LIKE CARS

They are convenient, comfortable, and they give us the freedom to go where we want, when we want (more or less). We like trucks, too, because they carry goods and services to the places where we need them, and make our lives easier. And cars and trucks aren't the only types of motor transport. We also have motorbikes, buses, trains, aircraft, and boats.

FACT!

More Americans own cars than any other people in the world, and use more petrol. The USA uses about 380 million gallons (about 1.44 billion litres) of petrol every day, that's more than a gallon for every man, woman and child in the country.

Traffic that is slow-moving or stuck in traffic jams produces huge amounts of **air pollution** on motorways and in towns and cities.

Lead away

Until the 1980s, petrol contained the metal lead, and burning it in motor vehicles added tiny particles of lead to the air. Lead is poisonous and it especially affects brain development in young children. Under pressure from campaigners, governments in many countries eventually banned the use of lead petrol in road vehicles – which just goes to show that we can change things when we try! However, lead petrol is still used in some off-road vehicles and in some countries.

The point is, most of our transport relies on burning oil in some form or another and, as we know, burning oil produces CO_2 and other GHGs – which leads to global warming. Globally, transport produces fewer emissions than energy supply, industry, deforestation, or agriculture. But that still makes it the fifth biggest emitter, and use of transport is still growing.

UNHEALTHY AIR

But that's not all. Burning petroleum also gives off other pollutants, such as the gases carbon monoxide, nitrogen oxides, sulphur dioxide and hydrocarbons, as well as dust and other bits of stuff known as **particles** (see page 63). All of these chemicals collect in the air and can cause us harm – such as shortness of breath, chest pains, asthma attacks and lung cancer. Polluted air affects animals, too, and causes **acid rain** (see page 60) which harms plant life. Of course, not all air pollution is due to transport. Burning any fossil fuel adds similar chemicals to the air. But in towns and cities where motor transport is widely used, it is often the biggest producer of air pollution.

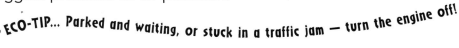

ECO-TIP... Parked and waiting, or stuck in a traffic jam — turn the engine off!

IT'S EXHAUSTING

Here's the really bad news. Exhaust fumes from all those cars that we love so much (and I'm including small vans here, too) account for about half of the world's CO_2 emissions from transport. Add in motorbikes and big trucks and the figure comes up to almost three-quarters.

In comparison, trains and buses produce a lot, lot less – because by sharing them we need far fewer of them. You can see what this is leading up to, can't you?

WE NEED TO CUT DOWN ON USING OUR CARS.

CARE MORE, CAR LESS

Many of us like our cars so much we use them all the time, even for very short journeys. Think what a difference we could make to the environment if everyone cut their car use by half, or even a quarter.

Walking or cycling short journeys keeps you fit, is more fun – you get to see what's going on in your neighbourhood – and is cheaper than driving. If you can't walk or cycle, catch a bus or train and feel good about the fact that you are helping the planet.

If you have to travel by car, maybe you could share your journey? If your parents drive you to school, for example, you could suggest they get together with your friends' parents and take it in turns to drive two or three of you in one car.

Cycling is good for you, and the planet!

The Netherlands has more **bicycles** than people, and the population cycles an average of about 900 kilometres per year, that's the equivalent of nearly 2.5 kilometres per person per day.

One of the problems with **aircraft** is that many fly high up in the atmosphere, and this increases the effect of some of the gases they give out.

FLYING HIGH

Apart from cars, the other fast-growing form of transport is aircraft. In many developed countries, some people jump on an aircraft in much the same way as they might hop on a bus or a train – to get to a business meeting, or for a weekend visit, or a holiday.

In terms of transport, aircraft are the third largest emitters of CO_2 and other gases after cars and trucks. Aircraft engineers are looking for ways to reduce aircraft emissions, but as long as planes burn jet fuel they will have an effect on the atmosphere.

Green campaigners would like everyone to **fly less**. They argue that many flights are unnecessary. Business meetings can take place on the internet, for example, and we could take holidays closer to home, or use the train and ferries.

IT'S ALL A QUESTION OF CHOICE.

Carbon offsetting

Carbon offsetting is a way of reducing business or personal GHG emissions by buying an 'allowance' for the 'carbon units' that are produced if you take a plane flight, for example, or use a lot of electricity. In return, the money you pay for the units goes to projects that help to decrease global warming and pollution.

Some say offsetting is wrong because it allows people to carry on polluting the atmosphere without taking responsibility for it and without changing their behaviour. Others say that offsetting works because it makes people aware of their emissions and puts more money into developing greener energy and other alternatives.

Hmmm! Planet or plane, planet or plane...

WHAT'S THE SOLUTION?

For now, cutting back on using motor transport will make a huge difference, but it is unrealistic to think that we will stop using cars, trucks and planes altogether. What we need is to find better ways to power them.

ELECTRIC CARS

Electric engines are already used in all sorts of vehicles. They are clean, quiet and efficient, but although they don't produce emissions themselves, the electricity they use is still mostly generated by burning fossil fuels. However, if they got their electricity from renewable energy sources, they could be the answer to our problems.

Most electric cars are **battery powered**, and the battery must be recharged every 80–160 kilometres. Plugging the car in at home is easy enough, but at present there are few public recharging points (above).

NATURAL GAS VEHICLES

NGVs, like this bus, use a form of natural gas that is mostly **methane**. Using natural gas in this way produces fewer emissions than petroleum. However, natural gas is non-renewable and, although cheaper than petrol, a tank of gas only goes about half as far as a tank of petrol. NGV cars are also more expensive to buy than petrol cars.

Mmmm, lovely hydrogen fuel cell waste! *

*i.e. water

HYDROGEN FUEL CELLS

One exciting possibility is **hydrogen** fuel cells. Amazingly, these turn hydrogen and oxygen gases into electricity, and the only 'waste' they produce is heat and water. However, although car manufacturers have produced test vehicles they are still too experimental for general use. Plus, at present, fossil fuels are burned to produce the hydrogen gas used in the cells. But, fuel cells could have other uses, too. Some scientists think that fuel cells might one day be used to generate emission-free electricity in power stations.

HYBRID CARS

One of the problems with electric cars is that they run out of power more quickly than petrol cars, so some companies are producing hybrid cars. These combine two **different types of power**, usually petrol and electric, and contain a tank for petrol as well as batteries for electric power. This means they produce less petrol emissions by using electricity for short journeys and only using petrol for longer trips, when refuelling is more easily available.

Which half has run out exactly?

HYB R1D

running on natural gas

FACT!

There are currently about 2.5 million NGVs worldwide, including taxis, buses and trucks.

BIOFUELS

These are made from plant or animal matter. The two main types are **biodiesel** and **bioethanol**. Biodiesel uses animal fats, or plant oils such as soybean or palm oil. Bioethanol is a type of alcohol and can be made from almost any plant material, such as corn, grass or wood. Biofuels are mostly mixed with diesel or petrol, although they can be used on their own. They are renewable, but there is a lot of debate about how much CO_2 they actually emit, and they do produce extra nitrous oxide emissions (see page 17). There are also concerns that using land to grow biofuel crops, such as oil palm (right), leads to deforestation, endangers biodiversity (see page 76), and adds to emissions from agriculture.

39

WHY ARE **TREES** IMPORTANT?

Trees give us one of nature's great materials – **wood**. Wood can be chopped into large chunks or split into tiny slivers. It can be made to bend or twist, it can be shaped, smoothed, carved and polished, or pulped and glued back together to make anything from floorboards to tissue paper.

For thousands of years we have burnt wood as a source of energy for heating, cooking and for industry, and used it as a building material for making homes, furniture, tools, musical instruments, boats, or just beautiful objects.

TREES FOR LIFE

Trees are also a fantastic source of food. They give us fruits, nuts, seeds, oils, sap, edible leaves and roots – and in many parts of the world they are a vital source of fodder for domestic animals, such as goats and cattle.

Trees, woodlands and forests support an enormous variety of other **wildlife**, from beetles and butterflies, to birds, mammals, fungi and flowering plants.

In remote places, trees may even supply the only forms of medicine for local people. Many of the medicines we now have originally came from tree products. Aspirin, for example, was developed from a chemical in willow bark. But trees have an even greater importance than giving us products we can consume, they are also vital to our whole environment.

When **forests** are cut down, the soil is often left bare. Rain washes the soil into rivers, heat from the Sun dries it out and turns it to dust, and wind blows it away. Any soil that remains quickly loses its goodness and its ability to grow anything.

TREES FOR THE PLANET

Tree roots spread through the soil and give it firmness and strength. They prevent the soil from being **eroded** (worn away) by wind, rain, or drought, and help it to soak up and store ground water. Trees provide shelter and protection for people and animals from extremes of heat or cold, and they affect the climate.

Trees – especially forests – help soak up carbon dioxide from the atmosphere. Their leaves remove CO_2 (and other pollutants, such as dust and ozone) during photosynthesis (see page 14), and store it in their wood, roots and leaves. For this reason, some environmentalists call forests **carbon sinks**. Of course, trees also give out carbon dioxide, through respiration and when they die and rot, but because forests usually soak up and store more carbon than they release, they help fight against climate change.

However, when trees are cut down and burnt, or they die through disease, or forests are destroyed to clear land, all the carbon they hold is put back into the atmosphere – which adds to climate change.

FACT!

Land soil and vegetation contain about three times as much carbon as the atmosphere, and forests contain over three-quarters of all the carbon that land vegetation holds.

In order to get to the trees, **logging** companies carve dirt roads deep into forests. Environmentalists say that when logging roads are cut, the remaining forest is over four times more likely to suffer deforestation than if there are no roads.

FOREST CLEARING

Woodlands and forests cover less than a third of the Earth's land. There used to be a lot more, but we have used wood for fuel and building for thousands of years, and cleared forests for land use. In the past, all trees were cut by hand and this still happens in some parts of the world. When people cut trees by hand, to use for themselves and their families, there is little wastage and the trees have time to replace themselves.

Trees are my best friends.

CUTTING MACHINES

Industrial logging, on the other hand, can strip whole hillsides in a few days. Logging machines often slice through everything above a certain height and so may destroy and waste up to ten times as many trees as are actually needed.

Many people now recognise that there has to be a better balance between nature's needs and the needs of people. It is vital to manage our remaining forests so that the amount of logging that takes place is controlled and trees are replanted. This approach is known as **sustainable** forestry, and includes planting new woodlands with fast-growing trees that are especially suitable for logging.

WHY DO WE CUT DOWN FORESTS?

Timber companies cut down trees to sell wood for things like furniture, flooring, and doors. The paper industry cuts down trees and mashes them into pulp to make toilet paper, cards, newspapers and cardboard. Wood is even burned in power plants – see 'Burning biomass' on page 44.

But forests aren't only cleared to supply wood. One of the major causes of deforestation is agriculture. Cattle farmers want more grazing land to raise more cows and sell more meat, and crop farmers want to grow and sell more crops.

Mining companies chop down forests as well, to get at the minerals underneath them, and entire forest valleys may be flooded for hydroelectric dams. Other people cut down trees to build roads through forests, and when the roads are in place, more land is cleared alongside them to build houses and businesses.

FACT!

The organisation Friends of the Earth says that we are losing our forests at the rate of an area the size of 36 football pitches every minute!

That's a lot of trees!

Lost and gone forever

More than half of the world's **rainforests** have already disappeared, and if we carry on clearing them at the same rate, they will all be gone in less than a hundred years – and it is not only the trees that are lost. Rainforests are home to about half of all known species of plant and animal life, and scientists believe they contain millions more still to be discovered (see page 76).

When the rainforests vanish, most of those species, like the orang-utans shown here, will vanish too – along with unique varieties of plants that could one day supply us with vital new medicines or other products.

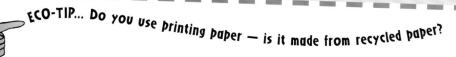

ECO-TIP... Do you use printing paper — is it made from recycled paper?

Burning biomass

Biomass is the name given to organic materials that are burned to generate electricity. Biomass fuels may contain waste, such as sewage, manure and food waste, but at present most biomass power plants burn wood. Some of this wood is also waste – leftovers from logged trees that cannot be used for anything else, for example, or wood from building or demolition sites. But biomass fuel often contains farmed trees and other plant crops that are grown especially for burning.

One argument for biomass fuel is that although burning it adds CO_2 to the atmosphere it adds a lot less than fossil fuels. Another is that because some types of trees and other plants can be grown quickly, biomass is a renewable fuel. However, one of the drawbacks is that land for growing biomass fuels may be found by cutting down and clearing away ancient forests.

FINDING A BALANCE

Governments and industries are beginning to learn from their mistakes and attempts are being made to control logging and to replant forests, although they could be doing a lot more! And other organisations are running campaigns to plant trees, too.

However, while growing trees is always a good idea, schemes to plant or replant forests on a large scale are not always successful.

The right types of trees have to be planted in the right kind of **habitat**, otherwise they fail and die – adding CO_2 to the atmosphere rather than taking it away.

Also, new trees do not hold as much carbon as old ones, or as great a variety of wildlife, so replacing ancient forests as part of a carbon-offset scheme, for example, or in exchange for more logging, can be just an excuse for not limiting CO_2 emissions or deforestation.

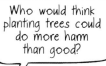

Who would think planting trees could do more harm than good?

SO HOW CAN WE BE FOREST FRIENDLY?

WE HAVE TO STOP DESTROYING OUR FORESTS!

My board is made from forest-friendly wood.

☀ Forests must be carefully managed so that only selected trees are cut and new ones are planted among the old.

☀ Governments can be pestered to control logging and other deforestation.

☀ Local people can be encouraged to report illegal logging and to harvest more food from their forests rather than clearing trees to grow crops.

☀ We can avoid buying food products grown on cleared rainforest land.

If you don't have a garden, or there's no room in it for more trees, find an organisation or charity that is **planting trees** in your neighbourhood, or country – or better still, in a country that may need trees more than you do.

☀ We can also be more careful about the wooden products that we buy. Look for recycled or sustainable wood – whether it's a birthday card or a surfboard.

Sustainable wood should carry a label to say it has been certified by an organisation such as the FSC (Forest Stewardship Council). This means the wood has come from a properly managed forest.

Remember, too, that things made of wood can often be mended, or recycled and reused – see pages 74–75 for more on recycling – and, last but not least...

GO OUT AND PLANT A TREE OR TWO... OR MORE.

HOW DID IT GET SO BAD?

The planet is in trouble and we know that we are causing it, so why don't we just stop?

TOO MANY PEOPLE

Well, one reason is that there are lots of us and we all want the same things – a place to live, food to eat, clean water, medicines when we get ill, and some way of working to pay for it all.

In the last two hundred years, the number of people living on Earth – its **population** – has exploded. In the early 1800s, there were less than 1 billion (one thousand million) people in the world. Today, there are nearly 7 billion (seven thousand million).

A BETTER LIFE

Most of this growth is due to scientific and technological improvements. We now have better farming methods, fertilizers, pesticides and agricultural machinery, and so we can grow more food than ever before.

We have better housing, with heating and proper sanitation (clean drinking water and disposal of sewage), so we have less disease and better public health. And we have made huge improvements in medicine and the treatment and prevention of disease.

All of which means that, worldwide, fewer children die at birth or from childhood diseases, and people have a longer life expectancy. In other words, more of us are born every week than are dying – and that means the population rises.

FACT!

About 2.5 million babies are born every week in the world, that's more than 4 babies every second.

The more the merrier!

What to expect

The average **life expectancy** worldwide (which means the average number of years a person is generally expected to live) is currently 65 years – twice as long as it was 100 years ago. But life expectancy varies – from person to person, but also from place to place. In developed countries such as Australia and the USA average life expectancy ranges from about 75 to 82. In many parts of Africa, however, it is as low as 38 to 50.

FACT!

Between 1950 and 2000, the world population increased from 2.5 billion to 6 billion. In the next 50 years, it is expected to reach more than 9 billion people.

BETTER FOR SOME...

However, all these improvements come at a cost. To provide them we have to use the Earth's **resources** – its land, seas, rivers, lakes, plants, animals, metals and minerals. This was fine when there were fewer of us and our lives were simpler, but more people and more technology means using more and more resources.

Also, as life has improved, people have come to expect better homes, more variety and choice of food, clothing and other products, and all the services our modern towns and cities provide. Or at least some people have.

The fact is, that if all of us lived this way there would not be enough resources to

In developed countries, farmers use motorised machines to help them work. In less developed countries most small farmers still do the work by hand or with the help of their farm animals.

go around (see 'How Many Earths?', page 19). So what actually happens is that the developed countries have grown wealthy using the biggest share of the world's resources, while in less developed countries many people do not have enough food, water, housing, medicine, education or access to modern technology.

ECO-TIP... Got a dripping tap? One drip per second wastes 20 gallons of water a day.

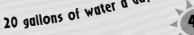

City living

More than half the people in the world today live in towns and cities – and about 1 billion of them live in slums. People move to cities to look for work when there is none in the countryside, but often the work they find does not pay them enough to afford proper housing. Instead they build themselves lean-tos and shacks out of waste wood, plastic and cardboard, although most lack safe supplies of water, sanitation, heating, or electricity.

...BUT NOT FOR ALL

In spite of our new and improved farming methods, over a billion people in the world do not have enough to eat. Most live in parts of Africa and Asia, but in every region of the world, even in developed countries, some people go hungry every day.

Nearly a billion people do not have regular supplies of clean water to drink, and 2.5 billion people live without proper sanitation, which leads to illness, disease and death.

Although there have been enormous advances made in health care and medicine, more than 8 million children a year still die before the age of five – almost all of them in less developed countries, and most from preventable causes.

FACT!

More than 20 billion US dollars is spent on pet foods in Europe and the USA each year. It has been estimated that it would cost about 17 billion US dollars to feed all the hungry people in the world.

Do you think we should donate some of our food?

MAKING IT WORSE

There are already huge differences between rich countries and poorer countries in the way people live – and climate change will make it worse.

Rising sea levels and more storms will flood many coastal areas, making it impossible for people to live there or use the land for farming. At the same time, other parts of the world will become drier and suffer from drought, also making farming impossible and the land uninhabitable.

Countries that previously grew food to sell to other parts of the world will no longer be able to do so, which means that there will be less food available so it will become more expensive.

PUTTING ON PRESSURE

Because developing countries tend to have large populations but little money to spend on them, they will be the worst affected by these changes.

And when people cannot find work or food where they live, they are forced to move (migrate) to other places to search for it. Often this means that they head for towns and cities, putting more pressure on parts of the world that are already overcrowded.

With an ever-expanding population using ever-decreasing resources, it is clear why groups, such as the WHO (World Health Organisation), are saying that it is time to take urgent action.

With **floods** on the increase, especially in Bangladesh and other parts of Asia, some scientists think that we are already starting to see the effects of climate change.

SO WHAT CAN WE DO?

We know climate change is the biggest problem, because it will affect everything else in our lives, and we know we have to reduce GHG emissions to stop climate change getting worse. But we also need to do other things, too.

We need to find ways of sharing the planet's resources more fairly, and that means that the people who are living in the wealthier, more developed countries need to be willing to give up some of their wealth – so that others can have a little more. It won't be easy, but one way we can start is to **change the way we think** about our world.

We need new thoughts for a brighter future!

How wealthy are you?

Okay, so if you live in a developed country (and the fact that you are reading this book means you probably do), you may be thinking that you are not very wealthy. After all, you don't live in a big house, or buy lots of expensive things, or go on lots of holidays.

But, if you...

can choose the food you want to eat	can choose the clothes you want to wear	sleep in a warm and comfortable bed at night	go to school and know how to read and write	have a TV/mobile phone/games console

...you live a life that is wealthy beyond the dreams of the other half of the world's children that live in poverty.

YOU CAN TRY TO...

☀ **Support a charity** that works to relieve poverty and hunger, such as Oxfam, Action Aid or Save the Children. This doesn't only mean giving them your money or unwanted clothes. Charities like these only exist because people are willing to work for them for free. If you have any spare time, you could volunteer to help. Or you and your friends could organise an event for the charity, which would raise money and make more people aware of what the charity is doing – and why.

☀ **Learn** about what is happening to people in poorer parts in the world – and then share what you have learnt. The more of us that understand the problems faced by others, the more we may be able to find ways to help them.

Although India is working hard to increase its industry and wealth, it has more **hungry children** than anywhere else in the world.

Smaller families

Many experts believe that no matter what we do there is a limit to how many people the world can support. The only answer is to stop the population increasing, and that means having fewer children. In many developed countries people already have fewer children and population figures are staying the same or are falling. But in most developing countries, people are not able to choose whether or not to have children, or how many to have, and so their population figures are continuing to rise.

☀ **Write to your government** to say that you want them to do more to help prevent poverty and hunger. Most of the developed nations already send money and other aid to poorer countries – but even more than aid, these countries need help to gain the knowledge, skills and equipment that would allow them to create more jobs, better businesses and a better life for their people.

You will also find more suggestions for other things you can do in the next chapters.

ECO-TIP... Buy one thing less each week and give the money you save to charity.

WHY DO SOME PEOPLE GO HUNGRY?

One billion people,

that's one in every six people in the world,

do not get enough to eat

– yet it is possible for the world to produce enough food for everyone, so why are some people starving?

When there is a **famine** in one country, other countries usually give aid in the form of food or money. But if the famine goes on for a long time, or there are more famines in other parts of the world, the aid can run out.

IT'S A DISASTER

Well, sometimes there are natural causes, such as floods or storms, or when there is not enough rain. Then crops fail to grow and cattle and other livestock die. Natural disasters like these tend to happen more in some parts of the world than others – and when they happen in developing countries in Asia or Africa, for example, they can lead to famine.

BUYING AND SELLING

All countries buy and sell food, otherwise people in Europe would not eat bananas, for example, and people in Africa would have very little wheat. But some developing countries rely heavily on selling food crops. When their crops fail they not only have less food to eat, they have less to sell and so do not have enough money to buy food from other places.

RISING PRICES

When there is less food available, the price of it goes up. In recent years, natural disasters have been on the increase because of climate change – and not only in developing countries. Australia has had a severe drought for the past few years, for example, affecting its food production and adding to world shortages.

When fuel costs more, so does food.

FUEL
FOOD

Food prices also rise when the cost of producing the food goes up. In many places, fuel energy is used to grow, process and transport food, and when fuel costs rise – which they will as long as we use fossil fuels – the cost of food rises too. All of which makes it harder for poor people to get enough to eat, even when there is food in the shops.

FOOD FOR FUEL

Unfortunately, our search for renewable fuels can make things worse. More and more farmland is now being used to grow crops for biofuels (see page 39), and while this may help our energy supplies it makes food shortages worse.

Edible crops such as corn, soya beans and sugar cane are now increasingly being turned into fuel. About one third of all of the corn grown in the USA is used for biofuel, for example, and both Brazil and China have switched millions of acres of farmland to growing biofuels.

War on food

Another major cause of food shortages and famine is wars and fighting. Over the last twenty years, millions of people have had to flee their homes and land because of armed conflicts in parts of Africa and Asia. Wars destroy property, crops and livestock as well as people. Sometimes the destruction is accidental and sometimes deliberate as warring armies try to wreck their opponents' food supplies. And the destruction can last long after the armies have moved on. Water sources may be permanently polluted and fields littered with explosive land mines, making it impossible for farmers to return to their land.

ECO-TIP... Buy fresh food rather than frozen – frozen food uses up more energy.

In the USA in the 1930s, a combination of drought, **over-farming** and wind storms turned millions of acres of once fertile farmland into dust.

A GROWING PROBLEM

Then there is the way we grow our food. Although improvements in farming mean that we can now grow and harvest more food than ever before, there is a downside.

Using fertilizers to help crops grow, and sprays to kill pests and diseases guarantees bigger and better crops, but pollutes our air, water and soil, (see pages 63–67). And when soil is made to grow crops too quickly it can become exhausted and lacking in nutrients which makes it unable to grow anything at all. When crops fail, people and animals starve and the soil turns to dust, leaving it open to **erosion** by wind and rain.

Also, clearing land to grow crops for business or biofuels, or as grazing land for cattle ranches, is a major cause of deforestation and loss of habitats such as grasslands. This not only affects wildlife but can mean that local people are no longer able to use the land as a source of food for themselves.

The cost of farming

Farming crops and livestock uses about 40 per cent of the world's land and 70 per cent of its usable water. It is the biggest single consumer of land and water than anything else we do.

Agriculture is also the biggest producer of the gases, methane and nitrous oxide, and the fourth biggest producer of GHG emissions in total after energy, industry, and changes to land use (which includes deforestation) – and it is one of the major reasons for changes in land use.

Watering crops

A RICH DIET

People in wealthy countries eat a lot of meat, and as countries such as China and India become richer more people there will be able to afford to eat more meat as well. In the next twenty years, the number of farmed animals is expected to double. Livestock already account for one-third of GHG emissions from farming (see page 16), so producing more meat will only make this worse. Raising cattle also uses more land and water than growing vegetables and grains, leaving less available for these crops and creating more food shortages. Luckily, the answer to this is easy.

We all need to eat less meat, especially if we live in the developed countries! And while we're on the subject of eating less…

Yum! Veggies are scrummy!

SLURP! SCRUNCH!

WHAT A WASTE

Even though there are food shortages, famines, erosion and land loss, people in the developed countries have more cheap food than ever before.

Most of this is due to the buying power of the big supermarkets and food processing companies, who order such enormous amounts of food that they are able to get it very cheaply. But having lots of cheap food encourages us to buy more than we need – making us unhealthy and overweight, and creating mountains of waste. Shops, restaurants and families in developed countries all throw out millions of tonnes of usable food each year and most of it ends up in landfills (see page 70).

In the poorest countries, people spend as much as half to three-quarters of their money on food. In wealthy countries it can be less than a quarter.

FACT!

People in the USA put one-third of their edible food in the dustbin – and it is not all scraps and leftovers, but food that is perfectly good, just not wanted.

Okay, let's see what's on the menu tonight?

SO LET'S GO FISHING

Of course, farming is not our only source of food. The world's oceans are stuffed with thousands of varieties of fish – all there for the taking. Or are they? That was true once upon a time, but not any longer.

Fishing trawlers like these are now so efficient at catching fish there soon won't be any left to catch.

As with farming, technological improvements over the past 100 years have led to bigger and better boats catching more and more fish – and now we are running out. Research from scientists shows that if we go on grabbing everything we can from the oceans as we are doing now they will be virtually empty in 50 years' time.

THERE ARE ALTERNATIVES

For example, we could set up ocean sanctuaries, similar to wildlife reserves in Africa, where people are only allowed to fish selectively, or not at all. At present, only a tiny part of the oceans is protected from over-fishing. But scientists have discovered that fish do restock themselves in these areas, as long as it is not left too late.

However, protecting the oceans on a large scale will only work if every country, and its fishermen, agree to keep to the rules. This would mean fewer fishermen and many people would lose their jobs – but the fish and the oceans could be saved!

SUSTAINABILITY

It also helps if we eat **sustainable** fish. This is fish that is either farmed, or caught by methods that do not damage the fish stocks or the environment.

Farmed fish are grown and fed in special enclosures instead of living in the wild. However, at the moment, fish

Fish farming can help our food supply, but not if it endangers wild fish.

Ask your parents to only buy fish that has the Marine Stewardship Council (MSC) label. This shows that the fish comes from a sustainable source.

farming needs improving as it can pollute open waters nearby, which then affects the wild fish, but it does supply more fish for food and takes the pressure off wild fish.

Of course, both solutions depend on climate change not making everything worse by altering the temperature and chemical balance of the oceans.

Yep, we're back to climate change, again!

Where's the water...

Almost three-quarters of the Earth's surface is covered in water, yet only a tiny amount of it is fresh water and usable by humans. This ought to be enough, but because of climate change, pollution, population growth, and increasing water usage, millions of people do not have clean drinking water and live in homes without proper toilets and sewage. About 4,000 children die each day from diarrhoea caused by bad water and no sanitation.

Top eco-water tips

It takes a lot of energy to pump, filter, and supply fresh water – and using all that energy produces emissions. Saving water and wasting less costs less money and is better for the environment.

Always turn off taps, never leave them running while you are doing something else.

Spend a minute or two less in the shower.

Don't run the tap to get a glass of cold water, keep a jug or bottle in the fridge.

Take a bucket into the shower and use the water it catches to water garden or house plants.

If you have ice cubes left in your drink, give them to a plant.

Ta!

CAN'T SOMEONE INVENT SOMETHING?

You might think that as scientific improvements helped get us into this mess, scientists should help to get us out of it. The problem is that, as we have learned, new inventions can bring unexpected changes in the future.

One thing that scientists are doing is looking for ways to make food plants stronger and more able to survive in worsening climate conditions. This means developing plants that can grow in dry conditions, for example, or in saltier soil along coastlines. Or that need less fertilizer to make them grow, or fewer pesticides. Some scientists are even trying to produce meat without rearing animals.

Hmm! Think I'll call it Instalamb!

ZAP!

Good as gold?

Up to half a million children in developing countries go blind each year through lack of vitamin A in their diet. GM scientists have developed a new type of rice called 'Golden Rice', which contains about 20 times as much vitamin A as other rice. However, some people say that Golden Rice is not the solution. Instead, more should be done to make sure that children get enough of the right variety of foods to give them all the vitamins they need.

NEW FOODS

Changing food plants and creating new types of food in this way is called **genetic modification**, or GM for short. Some people are afraid of GM foods and worry that these changes could damage our health or the environment in the future. Others say that farmers have been changing and improving our food crops for years and it makes no difference if it is done in a laboratory or in a field.

For better, or worse, however, it is clear that GM foods can make a difference to the quality and amount of food we can grow.

CUPBOARD LOVE

ECO-TIP... Try not to buy leather farmed in the Amazon.

But science cannot give us all the answers. To make the right decisions about what we eat, we need to know how our food is produced, and where it comes from. And we should remember that food and water are precious resources.

And we can try to...

Now let's see, where does this lot come from?

☀ Think more carefully about the food we buy – and waste less of it. It would also help if we made even small changes to our diet. Eating more vegetables and giving up meat even once or twice a week, for example, and choosing sustainable fish.

☀ Buy local food whenever we can, which is grown in the right season. When we do buy food from other countries we could try to support small farmers working in poor countries. At the moment, the best way to do that is to buy products that carry the FAIRTRADE Mark on them.

It's a fair trade

Fairtrade is about making sure that small-scale farmers and workers in developing countries receive a fair price for their products and an additional amount, the Fairtrade Premium, which farmers and workers can invest in projects to improve the lives of their families and communities. Fairtrade products always carry the FAIRTRADE Mark.

FACT!

Three-quarters of the world's footballs are made in Asia by people who are paid almost nothing to hand-stitch them. Many of them are children, working up to 11 hours a day. Next time you buy a football, make sure it has a FAIRTRADE Mark so you know that the person who made it has got a better deal.

BOY, HAVE WE MESSED UP!

Humans are a messy bunch, and the more of us there are, the more mess we make. Along with climate change and population growth, our other big problem is **pollution**. Pollution means adding something that is harmful or poisonous to the environment – and we've been doing a lot of that.

FUELLING POLLUTION

You already know how fossil fuels are causing climate change, but burning fossil fuels pollutes our planet in other ways too. The mixture of gases released into the atmosphere poisons our air and damages our health (see page 35), and when these gases are picked up by tiny droplets of water in clouds they turn into something called **acid rain**.

RAINING DOWN

The important word here is 'acid'. Acid is a chemical that burns or dissolves other materials, even metal. Acid rain contains a very weak form of acid, but over time it damages soil, trees and other plants, and pollutes water. It can kill whole forests and turn lakes into dead zones where nothing can live.

Weather carries acid rain from one country to another, and governments around the world are realising that in order to prevent it they have to work together to produce fewer emissions. Some countries are building power stations that burn fuels more cleanly – but the only long-term solution is to find greener sources of energy.

FACT!

Acid rain doesn't have to be rain, it can be fog, snow, hailstones or even dust. Scientists use the term 'acid rain' to mean any polluted form of water or particles that fall from the sky.

I don't think this umbrella is going to help!

If we die out, they do too!

Humpback whales have been hunted almost to extinction, now the **plankton** they eat is under threat from our pollution.

MAKING HOLES

Then there are those 'holes' in the ozone layer (see page 17), caused by using CFCs in sprays and plastics. Even though CFCs have largely been replaced by other halocarbon gases, some of them are not very ozone friendly either. And because they stay in the atmosphere for a long time it is likely to be another 60 to 70 years before the ozone layer recovers.

In the meantime, more ultraviolet (UV) rays from the Sun reach Earth. UV rays damage our eyes and cause skin cancer. In large amounts they can destroy land plants, including food crops, and they kill off plankton, the tiny animals and plants that float in the sea. Whales, fish and many other sea creatures depend on plankton for food, so if the plankton disappears, so will they.

Foaming mad

Plastic foam, known as polystyrene, is made from petroleum. We use it for packaging and protecting all sorts of things from hot drinks and food to computers. The manufacture and use of polystyrene releases dangerous chemicals into the air and can cause severe health problems in people who come into regular contact with it. Various polystyrene products make up a substantial amount of the plastic waste filling up our land and our oceans (see pages 71-72).

ECO-TIP... Taking a packed lunch? Put it in a reusable box instead of plastic bags.

SMOG-ZONE

There may be too little ozone high up in the atmosphere, but we are collecting too much of it lower down, in the air that we breathe. Ozone does not form naturally at lower levels, it is produced when gases from burning fuels – especially petroleum – mix with other gases, such as methane and halocarbons (see pages 16-17), and are then exposed to sunlight.

Low-level ozone is a major ingredient of a type of fog known as **smog** that hangs in thick clouds over motorways and cities. It is harmful to our airways and lungs, and especially to people with asthma. Ozone also affects photosynthesis in plants, and limits their growth. Some countries have taken steps to reduce smog, but doctors believe that it still leads to thousands of deaths each year.

Smog can also be caused by smoke from power stations and factories. When particles in the smoke mix with water in the air they create a thick acidic fog. Some countries have laws limiting the release of smoke, but in developing countries such as China (above), dense smogs continue to form.

A killer cleaner

Aside from burning fuels, ozone is added to the atmosphere in other ways, too. Ozone gas can be dissolved in liquids and because it is great at killing bacteria, it is often used as a cleaner in hospitals and food factories and to disinfect water, for example. Photocopiers and laser printers also emit ozone when they print.

EEEEK!

PARTICULAR DUST

Dust is the name we usually give to all the tiny, solid bits of stuff that float in the air or collect on surfaces. Scientists say that dust is made up of **particles**. These particles might include little bits of soil, sand, salt, or pollen from plants, or they could be fibres from different materials, soot from burnt materials, or tiny amounts of gas or liquid chemicals.

Some particles are there naturally – the wind picks up soil or pollen, for example, or soot from forest fires, or dust from exploding volcanoes.

But a lot of particles are put there by humans – either by burning fossil fuels or manufacturing different materials, or by spraying crops with pesticides, and so on.

All of it adds pollution to the air, and most of it has bad effects on our health, causing heart and lung disease, skin problems, and shortening people's lives.

How you can help

✓ Avoid using any spray aerosol products. Although most no longer contain CFCs (see page 17), they may still include other damaging chemicals.

✓ Check labels for paints, glues, solvents and cleaning materials and try to avoid anything containing CFCs or VOCs (Volatile Organic Compounds).

✓ Don't buy or use plastic foam cartons, cups or packaging.

And, of course... use LESS energy and fewer fossil fuels!

  **FACT!**

Dust in the house is mostly made up of minuscule pieces of human skin, hair, fabric fibres and the waste matter of millions of these tiny creatures – **house mites**.

Spraying **pesticides** helps us improve the amount and quality of the food we grow – but the hidden price we pay is pollution.

KILLING PESTS

All the pollution hanging around in our air doesn't necessarily stay there. A lot of it drifts down onto the land, or is washed there by rain. This includes the hundreds of chemical pesticides we use to kill off things we think are harmful or dangerous to our food or us, such as weeds, insects, moulds, bacteria, slugs, worms, mosquitoes, wasps, ants, rats, even birds and fish.

HELPFUL...

Life would be tougher without pesticides. Mosquitoes spread diseases, like yellow fever and malaria, which kill thousands of people every year in Africa and other developing countries. Beetles and fungi eat away at houses and other buildings. Mice and rats attack our food stores, and insects and moulds destroy food crops.

AND HARMFUL

The problem is that most of these chemicals are poisons of one sort or another and can have long-term effects on human health, especially to farmers and agricultural workers. They also kill many more varieties of wildlife than they are intended for, especially if they build up in a **food chain**.

When some animals eat sprayed plants it does not necessarily kill them but poisons may collect in their bodies. When these animals are eaten by other animals, the predators take in the poisons in the first animals' bodies. The more animals they eat the more poison they absorb. And when we eat contaminated plants or animals, poisons collect in our bodies as well.

FACT!

In tests done in the USA, potatoes were found to contain a variety of 17 different pesticides.

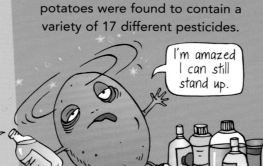

I'm amazed I can still stand up.

Deadly DDT

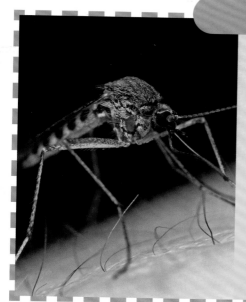

DDT is a very efficient and poisonous pesticide. During the 1900s, thousands of litres of it were used in countries all around the world. But by the 1960s, people became worried about the environmental damage DDT was causing, especially to birds such as eagles and falcons. DDT in their diet was causing the birds to lay eggs with thin shells that easily broke, so fewer healthy birds were born and their numbers were dropping dramatically. DDT was also found in fish and in the bodies of people who ate fish. Using DDT as an agricultural pesticide is now banned throughout the world, although it is used against mosquitoes, like the one shown here, and in spite of the ban it is still being used on food crops in some places.

IS IT ORGANIC?

Most countries control the amount and type of pesticides that can be used, although some have stricter controls than others. Even so, many people have become so worried about the effects of pesticides they have started to buy or grow food organically.

Organic farming means growing food in as natural a way as possible, without adding any (or as little as possible) manufactured chemicals in the form of pesticides or fertilizers. At first, organic farming was done in a small way, with people buying food directly from the farmer. Now most supermarkets stock organic foods and they are produced by large companies.

Some people argue that pesticides are necessary to provide the amount of food the world needs. Others say that organic farming can produce much the same levels of food as standard farming methods and the crops are more able to cope with difficult weather conditions. Also, that as well as producing less pollution, organic farming also produces fewer GHG emissions.

Organic vegetables are better for the planet!

Organic farming uses traditional methods alongside modern thinking.

WHAT'S IN THE WATER?

Of course, all this stuff – acid rain, dust, pesticides and so on – also ends up in our water. Rain washes it into streams and rivers, or onto the land where it soaks through the soil and drains into rivers and lakes that way.

Most of our usable water comes from rivers and lakes, or is pumped up through wells dug deep into the ground. Water that is contaminated by chemicals or human or animal waste causes illness, disease and death, which is why, in many parts of the world, the water we use is treated and purified beforehand.

However, this means using more chemicals to kill the germs that may be in the water, as well as machines (energy) to pump and filter it. At the moment, not every country can supply enough clean water for all its people.

SPRINGING A LEAK

Then there is the oil, gas or waste chemicals that leak into the ground or water from storage tanks, and the liquids that seep out of landfill sites where waste has been buried (see page 70). Plus, in some cases, the chemical waste that is deliberately dumped into land or water by companies just trying to get rid of it.

After 100 years of industrial development, most parts of the world contain some areas of seriously contaminated soil or water, and while they are being cleaned up in one place, more are building up somewhere else.

> Yuck! I wouldn't fancy swimming in that!

A huge amount of land pollution eventually ends up in the sea. Chemicals from fertilizers used on farms and gardens cause thick **mats of scum** and algae to form on the surface of the ocean, using up oxygen and suffocating ocean wildlife.

ECO-TIP... Don't put old medicines in the bin or down the toilet — take them to a chemist

WHAT'S THE ANSWER?

Some pollution can be cleaned up, but it is not always completely successful.

Air, water or soil can be filtered to remove pollutants – although these still need to be got rid of safely. Soil can be dug up and taken elsewhere – although it will carry on affecting the environment. Sometimes mixing bacteria with soil can help, or it can be buried and sealed to keep the contamination in.

You can't help thinking it would be better **not to put it there** in the first place!

The problem is, we can't just stop using chemicals. Many of them can save people's lives just as much as they can harm them. The best we can do right now is be more aware of the damage they can cause, and much more careful in how we use them and when. We can also carry on searching for better and less harmful alternatives.

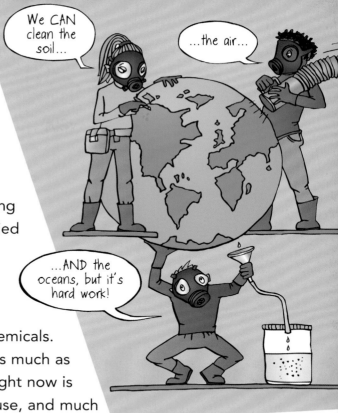

We CAN clean the soil...

...the air...

...AND the oceans, but it's hard work!

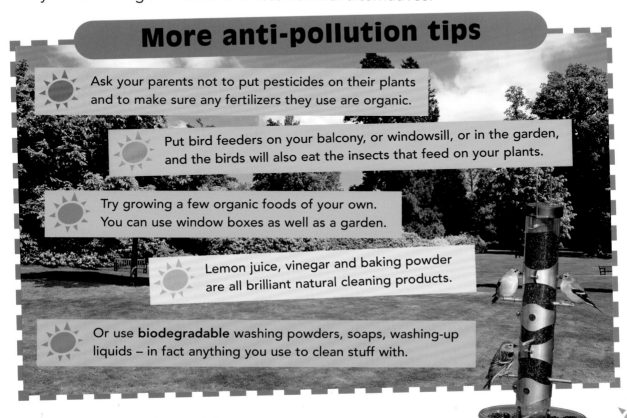

More anti-pollution tips

Ask your parents not to put pesticides on their plants and to make sure any fertilizers they use are organic.

Put bird feeders on your balcony, or windowsill, or in the garden, and the birds will also eat the insects that feed on your plants.

Try growing a few organic foods of your own. You can use window boxes as well as a garden.

Lemon juice, vinegar and baking powder are all brilliant natural cleaning products.

Or use **biodegradable** washing powders, soaps, washing-up liquids – in fact anything you use to clean stuff with.

WHAT A LOAD OF RUBBISH!

It's Saturday and you are hanging out with a bunch of friends. Along the way you picked up a few snacks – some crisps, fizzy drinks, the usual. When you've finished you crush the containers and…what? Put them in the nearest rubbish bin, of course.

Now imagine if everyone in the world did the same thing – that's 7 billion crisp packets and 7 billion drink cartons just in one Saturday afternoon. How big a rubbish bin would that need? Maybe one as big as a planet – because that is pretty much what is happening. We are turning the Earth into a gigantic, interstellar rubbish bin spinning in space.

Tonnes of hippos

To give you an idea of how much a tonne of rubbish is, think of an almost full-grown hippo – a sort of 'teenage hippo'. Now try to imagine 7.6 billion teenage hippos. That's more than one hippo for every single person on the planet, and that's just the industrial waste from one country for one year.

WASTING AWAY

Rubbish, or waste, is all the stuff we throw away – and there's plenty of it. Factories, mines, farms and power stations all chuck out billions of tonnes of solid, liquid and chemical **industrial waste** every year. A lot of it causes the pollution we looked at in the last chapter.

Of course, the more industries a country has, the more waste it makes. Currently, the USA is top of the world's industrial waste heap, producing around 7.6 billion tonnes of solid industrial waste a year.

BAGS OF RUBBISH

Then there's our household rubbish, and all the stuff collected from offices, shops, schools, hospitals, restaurants, parks, playgrounds and our streets. People in governments and the waste collection business call this **municipal waste**.

Worldwide, we produce about 2 billion tonnes or more of municipal waste each year, and it could rise to 3 billion tonnes by 2030. And, as usual, developed countries produce the largest share, especially of plastics, paper and metal.

FACT!

Wow! I've got to lose some weight!

On average, people in developed countries produce about 570 kgs of municipal waste per person per year. So if you weigh about 50 kgs, for example, you are throwing away more than eleven times your body weight in rubbish every year.

What's in your bin?

Household waste varies depending on where people live and how it is measured. According to the organisation WRAP, in general, household rubbish bins in the UK, for example, contain:

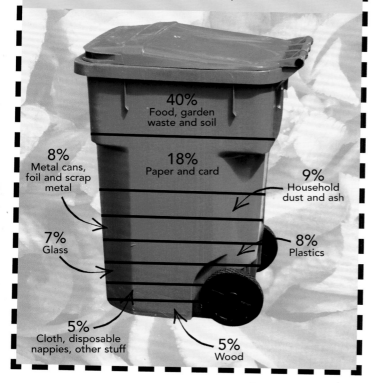

40%
Food, garden waste and soil

8%
Metal cans, foil and scrap metal

18%
Paper and card

9%
Household dust and ash

7%
Glass

8%
Plastics

5%
Cloth, disposable nappies, other stuff

5%
Wood

THE LIQUID STUFF

And don't forget **sewage** – municipal waste doesn't include sewage. That's all the water we use for washing our cars, dishes, clothes and ourselves, along with our body waste – our urine (pee) and faeces (poo). Plus there is industrial sewage, which is the liquid waste left over from different industrial processes.

Sewage needs to be disposed of carefully, as it can contain a soup of poisonous chemicals or various bacteria and viruses that give us diseases if they get into our food or drinking water.

ECO-TIP... Avoid using disposable plates, cups, cutlery, napkins, etc.

SO WHERE DOES IT ALL GO?

Waste disposal is an enormous problem for every country. In the past, most rubbish was just dumped onto the land. Even today, vast heaps of rubbish pile up on the outskirts of towns and cities in some countries. In others, waste is buried in huge holes in the ground called **landfill sites**.

FILLING UP

When a landfill site is full it is covered with a layer of soil and the rubbish is left to rot. But it's not as simple as it sounds. Rotting rubbish gives off toxic chemicals that can leak into the ground and poison water and plant life – and it produces tonnes of methane, which is a major greenhouse gas (see page 16).

An added problem is that as methane builds up in a landfill it can explode, so sites have to be carefully managed so that the methane is released.

Seagulls love landfills!

Rats do too!

Burying rubbish isn't a new idea. Humans have been doing it ever since they could walk and talk. The difference now is that there is so much of it. Countries in the European Union, for example, produce about 2 billion tonnes of waste each year, and over two-thirds of it goes into landfill sites.

FACT!

The UK has more than 4,000 landfill sites, producing an estimated 1.5 million tonnes of methane each year.

A BURNING ISSUE

If rubbish isn't buried it is sometimes burned. Burned waste mostly goes into large furnaces called **incinerators**. The good thing about an incinerator is that it reduces heaps of bulky rubbish to little piles of ash. It also destroys germs and poisons in some types of waste, such as medical waste for example.

The bad thing is that burning waste adds GHG emissions to the atmosphere. Modern incinerators can greatly reduce these emissions, and can even turn the heat they generate into electricity, which saves on using fossil fuels. But modern incinerators are expensive, and a great many older ones continue to pollute the air.

DOWN THE DRAIN

What isn't dumped, buried or burned, often goes down the drain. Millions of litres of liquid waste pours into the world's rivers, lakes and oceans every year. Some of it is filtered and cleaned to make it safe before it is dumped – but a lot isn't. As a result, some rivers and lakes have been poisoned for years to come.

Oil, fertilizers that have drained from fields, industrial chemicals, sewage, and all sorts of solid stuff ends up in the oceans – including lots of plastic. In fact there is so much rubbish in the oceans that an area of plastic junk as big as Texas (about 700,000 square kilometres) has been found floating in the Pacific Ocean.

The curse of the carriers

Each year the world carries home around 500 billion to 1 trillion plastic bags, and most of them end up in our rubbish. Plastic bags are everywhere, clogging up our land and oceans, and killing our wildlife. More than a million sea birds and other ocean animals die each year because of plastic rubbish in the oceans.

Stay free of the curse and say 'NO' to plastic carriers! Carry a reusable bag instead.

What did you get from the shops?

Some plastic bags!

THE PROBLEM WITH PLASTIC

Plastics are made from fossil fuels. They are strong, flexible, water resistant, can be moulded into any shape, and last for a very **long time** – and that's the problem! Plastic can take up to 1,000 years to degrade (break down), and when it does it breaks up into tiny, potentially harmful particles that get into our soil and water.

In the last fifty years or so we have thrown away about a billion tonnes of plastic, and most of it will still be with us at least 500 years from now. That's because plastic is almost impossible to get rid of. Burning it releases poisonous or polluting chemicals, and although some of it can be melted down and reused it is a difficult and expensive process.

FACT!

A report by the United Nations Environment Programme (UNEP) estimates that there are 13,000 pieces of plastic litter floating on every square kilometre of the world's oceans.

Wow! You mean I could leave this plastic bottle to my great, great, great, great, great, great, great, great, great, great, great, great, great, great grandchildren!

NOT SO BIODEGRADABLE

It is possible to produce plastic that degrades within a few years rather than a few hundred. But these **biodegradable** plastics are expensive to make, still use lots of energy to produce, and only break down in the right conditions.

Some environmentalists also worry that using biodegradable plastic encourages people to think that this type of plastic is not harmful to the environment when it still is.

Although biodegradable plastic is better than the other kind, unless we can come up with a type of plastic that is truly environmentally friendly the best thing of all is to use as little as possible, and reuse or recycle as much as we can of the plastic we already have.

WHAT ELSE CAN WE DO?

We all produce rubbish. We can't help doing it, it's just a fact of life. But we need to find better ways of dealing with it. One way is to stop thinking of it as rubbish, and start seeing it as another resource.

Getting rid of rubbish costs money, and many countries are now trying to improve their waste collection and disposal systems and find ways of making use of their rubbish.

WASTE ENERGY

For example, some solid organic waste can be burned directly as biomass to generate electricity (see page 44), and the gas given off by landfills can also be collected and burned to produce electricity. Other organic waste, such as sewage and leftover food can be broken down by bacteria to make more gas that can be used in this way.

Once organic waste has been broken down, any solids that remain can be put back into the land as natural fertilizer or compost.

Of course, another way is to make LESS WASTE in the first place!

DIY compost

If you have a garden, get your family to use their fruit and veg peelings, garden waste, teabags, coffee grounds, eggboxes and so on to make compost. It's not difficult to do and there are lots of websites and organisations that will tell you how. You can't compost all your food waste, but it will help lessen the load on landfills and your garden will love you for it. If you don't have a garden check with your local council to see if they recycle food waste.

Yummy! Compost!

ECO-TIP... Mop up spills with washable cloths, not kitchen towels.

LEARNING THE 3RS

Once upon a time, the 3Rs meant **Reading**, **'Riting** and **'Rithmetic**. Now they mean **Reduce**, **Reuse** and **Recycle**. The minute you look at the world from an environmental point of view it is pretty clear that a lot of us are using far more **stuff** than we need to – whether it's energy, water, food, plastics, clothes or cars. It is really important to start using less, and to make sure that we waste less of what we do use.

Now I know why I was bad at spelling.

 ## Here are a few ideas to get you started...

REDUCE...

☀ Use fewer materials more efficiently, for example, use both sides of the paper if you are printing stuff at home or school.

☀ If you know you won't be using something much, think about hiring or borrowing it before buying it.

☀ Join a book/music/film library and borrow stuff for free or for a small amount of money.

☀ Avoid packaging – for example, buy loose items and make your own sandwiches – or look for things that are wrapped in paper or cardboard.

☀ Granny had the right idea – use washable hankies instead of buying paper tissues.

REUSE...

☀ Repair or repaint things rather than replacing them with new all the time.

☀ Look for goods that are refillable or reusable rather than disposable, such as rechargeable batteries (especially if you can get a solar-powered recharger).

☀ Instead of throwing good stuff away, try selling it, or give it to your local charity shop.

☀ If you have to buy something, see if you can get it second-hand and save some money too.

☀ Reuse plastic tubs and glass jars to store leftover food instead of wrapping it in kitchen foil or clingfilm.

Charge it up

Each year millions of people buy millions of batteries. Batteries contain harmful chemicals and at the moment most of them end up in landfill sites. So don't chuck them in the bin, collect them up and look for a battery recycling point where you can hand them in. Or better still, use **rechargeable** batteries.

RECYCLE...

☀ As much as 80 per cent of what goes in your bin could be recycled. If you don't know already, find out how your local council recycles rubbish and get the rest of your family on board for recycling.

☀ When you buy any products look to see if they or their packaging can be recycled. If they can't, buy a similar product that can.

☀ Persuade your family to switch to buying products made of recycled material where they can – like recycled loo paper, for example.

☀ Remember that paper, metal, glass, wood and some types of plastic can be recycled – don't throw them in the bin, put them in a recycling container.

☀ Computers and mobile phones can be recycled too – find out how before you chuck them away.

Trash or treasure

There are some amazingly inventive ways of reusing things other people call rubbish. All sorts of recycled products are now available, from pencil cases made of tyres to backpacks and bags like these 'Doy Bags', made from foil and plastic drink cartons by women in the Philippines.

 ECO-TIP... Want something new to wear? Try swopping or sharing with a friend.

GOING, GOING... GONE!

In various places in this book I've said that climate change and pollution are affecting wildlife as well as humans, so this chapter explains a bit more about what that means and why it is such a bad thing.

A BIG MIX

When scientists talk about the number of different **species** of animals, plants and other life forms on Earth, they use the word **biodiversity**.

Biodiversity stands for biological diversity, or variety. It doesn't only mean all the different life forms on Earth, including us, it can also mean the different types that can be found within the same species, or even the different habitats species live in – from deserts or rainforests, to swamps or apartment blocks.

HOW MANY MILLIONS?

It may be a bit surprising, but no one actually knows how many life forms there are on Earth. So far, scientists have identified and named about 1.9 million separate species, but there could be anything from 5 to 10 million or more still to be discovered.

Most of the unknown species are likely to be insects, worms and other small creatures, but, as we are discovering, every life form has a part to play in the way the world works, no matter how small and unimportant they may seem.

WHAT BIODIVERSITY DOES FOR US

Grasses **feed** animals, provide all the cereals and grains we eat, and protect soil.

Bees **pollinate** flowers so plants can make more plants – and bees give us honey.

Owls, like this Barn Owl, **hunt** rats and mice. One pair of owls can kill more than 1,500 rats a year.

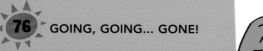

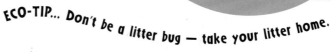
ECO-TIP... Don't be a litter bug — take your litter home.

Don't forget to add in the worms.

$33,000,000,000,000

A group of researchers have estimated that if humans had to pay for all of the services the natural world supplies to us, such as making soil, filtering water, regulating our air and climate, and so on, it would cost us something like 33 trillion US dollars a year (that's about £20 trillion, and a trillion is a million million).

AROUND AND AROUND

The parts of our planet that we depend on for life – air, water, and soil for growing food – in turn depend on living things to keep them working properly.

Green plants help balance the level of oxygen in the air, for example (see page 14). Bacteria and worms break down dead plant and animal material to make soil for plants to grow in. Plant roots hold the soil in place and prevent it being washed away by rain. Plants also protect the soil from heavy rainfall and help it to soak up rainwater, allowing water to be stored in the ground.

Dung beetles are some of the world's greatest **recyclers**. By burying animal dung, they improve the quality of soil.

Without oxygen and fresh water, plants and animals would die. Without plants, we and all the other animals would starve. And without animals, the soil would lose its nutrients and plants would be unable to grow.

And so it goes on…. In some way or another, everything relies on everything else in a vast and complicated cycle of life that developed over millions and millions of years and produced the amazing variety of life that we see around us. Until we came along and put a spanner in the works!

In spite of laws protecting gorillas, they are coming dangerously close to **extinction** – through hunting, the destruction of the forests in which they live, and infection from a virus that also affects humans and other animals.

MAKING CHANGES

Until now, humans have pretty much taken the world for granted. As far as we were concerned, the air, water and soil had always been there and would always be there. Plants and animals would go on supplying us with food and other materials just as they always had. And we could chop and change things around as much as we liked to make our lives more comfortable – or so we thought.

This may have been true when there were just a few million of us, but now there are thousands of millions of us and it is clear that the chopping and changing we are doing is threatening biodiversity, and all life on our planet.

GOING FAST

According to the World Wildlife Fund's Living Planet Index, the numbers of animals that belong to the species they are checking, are dropping fast – by almost one third in the last 40 years. And a report from the Millennium Ecosystem Assessment organisation estimates that species are becoming extinct 100 to 1,000 times more quickly than at any other time in Earth's history (see pages 8-9).

Visitors! How nice!

Dead famous

The Dodo was a strange-looking flightless bird that is famous as an example of how quickly we can kill off an entire species without meaning to. When humans arrived on the island of Mauritius in about 1600, they discovered the Dodo. They hunted it for food, but more importantly, they cut down the forests in which the birds lived. They also brought other animals with them – dogs, pigs, monkeys, cats and rats – and these destroyed the birds' nests. By the 1680s the Dodo had vanished.

THREATENING BEHAVIOUR

Conservationists – people who work to protect and preserve the natural world – believe that there are five main threats to biodiversity. Most of them are caused by the things we do.

Roads use up land and bring air and noise pollution.

1 LOSS OF HABITAT:

Caused by deforestation, changing grasslands into grazing or farmland, damming or draining rivers, building roads and houses, causing changes to coasts and oceans.

2 ALIEN INVASION:

No, not aliens from Mars, but plants or animals that move to a habitat where they are not naturally found, and take it over so successfully that other species cannot survive there. Most alien species are brought to new habitats by humans, either accidentally or deliberately.

Rabbits were taken from Europe to Australia in the 1800s, and have become a pest, destroying grasslands and young trees.

3 POLLUTION:

All the stuff we have been adding to the air, soil and water. You can read all about it on pages 60-67.

Industrial waste poisons our water, wildlife and us.

4 EXPLOITATION:

To exploit something means to make use of it – and it can mean to use it unfairly or selfishly and to over-use it, which is basically what we have been doing through over-hunting, over-fishing and over-using the world's resources.

The fish in our seas could all be gone in 50 years.

5 CLIMATE CHANGE:

By now you know quite a bit about climate change, and if rising sea levels and changes in climate and temperature are beginning to affect us you can imagine how other species will find it increasingly hard to survive.

Melting ice caps are endangering polar bears.

WHY DOES IT MATTER?

You might think that the loss of a few (or even a few hundred) species here or there wouldn't much matter.

But apart from putting our sources of food, water, materials and medicines at risk, we cannot possibly know which of the many species around us might prove to be vital to us in the future.

Mmmm, toxins!

Berkheya coddii is just one type of flowering plant that naturally soaks up toxic metals from the soil. Research is now being done into how growing and harvesting plants like these can clean up **polluted soil**.

SO WHAT CAN WE DO?

In 2002, most of the world's governments agreed to take action to substantially reduce biodiversity loss by 2010. However, although agreements were made, little real action was taken and the number of threatened species around the world continues to grow.

Making laws, and then making sure those laws are kept, can help to protect threatened species. However, if animals are hunted or habitats are destroyed because this is the only way that people can make money to feed themselves, then laws alone will not be enough. Governments also need to help people understand the effects of what they are doing, and develop other ways of earning money that will support and maintain them and their families – and their environment.

Oh, no! What can we do?

Hey, look at that!

WANTED: HAVE YOU SEEN THESE ANIMALS?

Hawksbill turtle — CRITICALLY ENDANGERED

Common hippopotamus — VULNERABLE

Cuban crocodile — ENDANGERED

Living museums

Zoos are a good example of our attitude to wildlife. The worst kinds of zoos cage up animals in poor conditions just for our entertainment. The best kind provide a protected environment for species that would otherwise be lost to the world, and they teach us about the value of those animals. Zoos rely on us to support them. It is up to us to decide which kind of zoos, if any, we would rather have.

It's good to be back!

Pere David's deer became extinct in the wild in the early 1900s. It is now being reintroduced into its natural home in China from animals that were bred in zoos in Europe.

FINDING A BALANCE

We know that the things that threaten biodiversity are also threatening us – and it is pretty obvious that the best solution for us and for the planet is to work **with the environment** rather than against it. For example:

☀ If we reduce greenhouse gas emissions, deforestation, waste and pollution, and control our population growth and share our use of resources more fairly, we can go a long way to reducing the loss of species at the same time.

☀ If we learn about the importance of biodiversity and the need to protect it, we can pass that knowledge on so that we stop losing so many species through ignorance.

☀ If we respect and pay attention to the needs of other species and learn to care for them rather than wastefully exploiting them – for example, if we stop emptying the oceans of its fish and other animals – we may even be able to stop losing species altogether.

It won't be easy, and it will take a great deal of time, money, hard work and belief from all of us – but in the long run, it is the only really practical and sustainable answer.

We'd better get started – don't you think?

We've got to get the balance right!

ISN'T ANYONE DOING ANYTHING?

Well, yes, quite a lot of people are in fact. From governments and politicians, to businesses, scientists, environmental organisations, artists, and individuals. But we still need many more of us to be doing more things – a lot more quickly.

Hssss!

GETTING A GRIP

Trying to get a grip on climate change is a bit like playing a game of Snakes and Ladders. At the same time that we are climbing up Ladders, by trying to reduce pollution and GHG emissions, the damage that we have caused and are still causing keeps sliding us down the Snakes again.

But, at least we are climbing the Ladders. After more than 50 years of arguing about it, most of the world's governments and their scientists do now accept that climate change is a serious threat caused largely by us, and that the only way to prevent an environmental catastrophe is to cut our emissions in half (see page 26).

It is not really so surprising that it has taken us so long. Climate change is a complicated issue and we have had a lot to learn. But in the time that we have taken to argue about it, things have got a lot worse.

FACT!

The first person to link a rise in global temperature with burning fossil fuels and the rise of carbon dioxide in the atmosphere was English engineer Guy Stewart Callendar, who wrote various scientific articles about it from 1938 until his death in 1964.

If we muck this up, there's nowhere else to go.

Astronauts on the Apollo 8 mission in 1968 took the first colour photographs of **Earth** from the Moon. Seeing Earth against the vastness of space made many people realise how small and fragile our planet is.

In the last 50 years...

 **1959**

World population reaches 3 billion – an increase of 1 billion people in 32 years.

 **1960s**

The use of pesticides, synthetic fertilizers and new types of wheat and rice seeds start to spread around the world. Known as the 'Green Revolution' it leads to a massive increase in food production – and in environmental pollution.

Aircraft crop-spraying pesticides.

 **1967**

Oil tanker, *Torrey Canyon*, runs aground off the coast of Cornwall in the UK, spilling thousands of tonnes of oil into the sea between England and France. This was the first of many big oil-spill disasters.

Torrey Canyon oil tanker breaks up.

 **1970**

Hungary, Norway and Sweden become the first countries to stop using DDT as a pesticide. In 2004, a UN agreement to ban its use as a pesticide came into effect.

 **1972**

The United Nations (UN) meet in Sweden for the first environment conference, and the United Nations Environment Programme (UNEP) is begun.

 **1985**

The British Antarctic Survey discover the first 'hole' in the ozone layer.

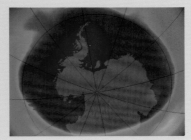

Thinning ozone over the Antarctic.

 **1987**

UNEP's 'Montreal Protocol' is signed by 24 countries agreeing to stop using CFCs because of their effects on the ozone layer. By 1995, CFCs were no longer in use in developed countries, although they will remain in the atmosphere for many more years to come.

 **1988**

The UN create the Intergovernmental Panel on Climate Change (IPCC) to research and report on global climate change.

 **1992**

At the UN's 'Earth Summit' in Brazil, over 150 countries agree to reduce CO_2 emissions, pollution and industrial waste.

Emissions from burning coal.

 **1997**

In response to further scientific warnings, the UN draws up the 'Kyoto Protocol', setting targets for industrialised countries to reduce their GHG emissions. The agreement came into force in 2005.

 **2009**

By the end of 2009, all the developed nations except the USA, and most developing nations except China and a few smaller countries, have confirmed their agreement to the Kyoto Protocol. However, few of the reduction levels promised in this agreement are being achieved.

ECO-TIP... Fridge frosted up? Improve its efficiency and defrost it.

WORKING TOGETHER

Recognising a situation and agreeing to do something about it is just the beginning. The hard part is actually doing it! One big stumbling block is that it requires all the countries in the world, especially the industrialised countries, to work together – and we are not always very good at doing that.

It is part of human nature to want to protect and provide for our own family, village, city or country first – and for much of our past that is what we have done. But (aside from nuclear warfare) the unique thing about climate change is that the changes it is bringing affect the entire planet.

For possibly the first time in human history we have to start caring about the whole planet in the same way that we care about our family and friends, neighbourhood and country. And to do this we have to try to ignore our differences and get together.

The speed the ice is melting is really scary!

Because of global warming, the ice at the Poles is melting twice as fast as 40 years ago. Sea levels all around the world are rising and could be as much as a metre higher by 2100.

MAKING AGREEMENTS

This is where the United Nations (UN) comes in. It is the one organisation that can bring all our countries together to talk about what is happening around the world, and to try to get them to agree what to do about it.

As a result of the 'Earth Summit' in 1992, the UN has held a world conference on climate change every year since 1995. The purpose of these conferences is to share information on climate change, and to search for ways to both tackle it and adapt to its impacts. Also to make sure that developed countries help and support the developing countries, which will be hardest hit by climate change.

AIMING AND MISSING

But it is a slow process. Because most of the world's GHG emissions come from developed countries, many of them agreed to reduce their emissions and set themselves targets for doing so. However, the targets they have set are still a long way below the level that climate scientists say is needed if we are to avoid a global temperature increase of more than 2°C (see pages 10-11).

On top of which, so far it appears that, although some countries have reduced their emissions to some extent, none are meeting their proposed targets and some have even increased their emissions.

United we stand

The United Nations was set up in 1945 after World War II. Its purpose was to prevent such a war from ever happening again by bringing the countries of the world together to discuss their issues or disagreements. Its headquarters is in the USA, but no single country governs the UN and it has many departments and offices around the world, including the World Health Organisation (WHO), the World Food Programme (WFP), and the United Nations Environment Programme (UNEP).

The UN is a major force for transferring help, medicine, food and water from wealthy parts of the world to countries in need.

ECO-TIP... Do you leave your phone charger plugged in? Turn it off at the socket.

TIME TO CHANGE

Scientists believe that we are running out of time in which to stop the climb of greenhouse gases and allow them to start falling back to a more normal level. They say that if emissions **don't start falling by 2015**, we will not be able to prevent major environmental disasters from happening.

This means that our governments have some tough decisions to make. They need to bring in stronger and more effective laws on energy and transport use, deforestation and other land change, overfishing, waste, and industrial and agricultural pollution. But at the same time, they must do their best to feed and house a global population that is expected to continue growing until at least 2050.

And to do this, they need industries and businesses to support them.

NEW IDEAS

Finding new ways of doing things costs money. Building alternative energy sources, or discovering better ways of using and reusing materials, for example, can only happen if a country has

FACT!

According to UNEP, buildings are responsible for more than one third of all energy use, greenhouse gases and waste generation.

enough money to spend on researching and developing these ideas.

Countries make their money from the businesses and industries that operate inside them. Both from the products and services those businesses and industries make and sell, and from the people who work in them.

We need more new ideas NOW!

The growth of new businesses and industries in the last hundred years has caused many of the problems we now face – but with the right ideas, it can also give us the solutions to those problems.

LET'S ALL GO GREEN

In 2009, UNEP produced a report called a 'Global Green New Deal'.
They asked for more countries to put more money into five key areas:

1 To make new and old buildings more efficient in the way they use heating and cooling, lighting, water and so on.

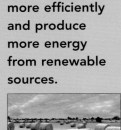

Insulating an attic stops heat escaping through the roof.

2 To provide energy supplies more efficiently and produce more energy from renewable sources.

Biomass products, such as straw, can be used to make energy.

3 To increase the development and use of cleaner and more sustainable methods of transport.

Electric trams in towns are a quiet and clean form of transport.

4 To encourage more sustainable methods of food production and water use, such as developing organic farming.

Less than 1 % of farm land is currently used to grow organic crops.

5 To protect and strengthen our ecosystems, such as the world's grasslands and rainforests, soils, rivers and oceans.

Coral reefs feed and shelter fish and protect shores from erosion.

An important part of UNEP's Green New Deal is also that the wealthier developed countries give more assistance to the developing countries to help them grow their energy supply, businesses and industries in a green way.

In India and Bangladesh, organisations provide villages with low-cost **solar panels**, and train local people to operate them. The panels improve people's lives by supplying a pollution-free, sustainable source of energy.

GREEN AT WORK

Many green businesses already exist, and more and more people are also trying to make the non-green companies they work for aware of their effect on the environment and help them operate more sustainably.

For example, people who produce solar panels or wind turbines, or work in recycling, organic farming, or wildlife conservation, are all doing green jobs and working for the benefit of the planet as well as for themselves.

IT'S UP TO US

You may not think it, but in the end governments and businesses react to the demands that the general public (that's you and me) make on them.

By our attitudes and actions, we can either support or oppose them. So it is up to us to let our governments and our businesses know that we want them to take action to reduce climate change and pollution, and to protect biodiversity. Even though this will mean we have to accept changes to the way we live now.

TAKING ACTION

One way of doing this is by supporting one or more of the non-government

The **World Wildlife Fund** was set up in 1961 to work for the protection and conservation of nature. It now has over 6 million members and works to defend and improve wildlife areas and species at risk, such as the last 4,000 wild tigers remaining in the world.

organisations that campaign for green issues. Most of these organisations are charities, which means they are set up and run by committed individuals, and rely on people to give them money in order to keep operating.

They may be local, national, or international, and may concentrate on a single issue – such as saving one species of animal or recycling one type of waste – or work on behalf of all environmental issues. Many of them carry out vital research and provide governments and the UN with a great deal of information, ideas and criticism.

The best way to get involved is to find an organisation that is working on an issue you want to support and offer them your help.

Greenpeace has about 3 million members worldwide, and campaigns on many environmental issues. Greenpeace ships like this one, for example, patrol the seas looking out for illegal fishing or ocean pollution.

ECO-TIP... Does your school save energy and recycle? If not, see what you can do.

CHOOSING A BETTER WAY TO LIVE

The other vitally important thing we can do is take direct action ourselves in whatever way we can to **reduce and limit** our impact on the environment. It may be hard giving up some things, or putting in the extra effort or time that it takes to live a more sustainable life, but it is far, far better for us to do it now, and by choice, than to be forced into it in a world that is collapsing around us.

There are ideas and eco-tips throughout this book, but even if you follow just these five you will make a difference.

5 BEST WAYS TO MAKE A BIG DIFFERENCE

Turn off lights and cut down on energy use.

Cycle, walk or use public transport rather than cars.

Stop using plastic bags.

Eat less meat and fish.

Don't waste water.

AND HERE'S THE GOOD NEWS

Changing the way we live and work could bring all of us huge benefits in terms of our health and wellbeing. It will bring us cleaner air and a better diet, protect us, our environment and our wildlife from deadly poisons, and help us to appreciate and enjoy the miracle that is our planet Earth…

AND THAT'S THE POINT OF BEING GREEN!

ORGANISATIONS & WEBSITES

☀ **Act on CO2** – UK government website on climate change, what the government is doing about it, and tips on what you and your family can do. http://actonco2.direct.gov.uk/actonco2/home.html

☀ **EIA Energy Kids** – US Energy Information Administration's website on everything to do with energy, its history, energy sources and uses. http://tonto.eia.doe.gov/kids

☀ **Energy Efficiency and Renewable Energy** – US Department of Energy website, for tips on saving energy click the 'What's Your Excuse?' link; for facts and games see 'Kids Saving Energy'. www.eere.energy.gov

☀ **EPA (United States Environmental Protection Agency)** – for info, links and games to do with weather and climate change go to EPA's kids' site: http://epa.gov/climatechange/kids/index.html

☀ **Footprint Friends** – a website to raise awareness about environmental issues for 10-18 year olds. www.footprintfriends.com

☀ **Friends of the Earth International** – campaigns on behalf of environmental and social issues around the world. http://www.foei.org

☀ **Global Action Plan** – a charity giving information and ideas to communities, businesses, schools and young people on reducing the effects of climate change. http://www.globalactionplan.org.uk

☀ **Greenpeace** – a campaigning organisation working to protect the environment and promote peace. www.greenpeace.org/international

☀ **Hooper Virtual Paleontology Museum**, Carleton University, Ontario, Canada – click on 'HVPM Gallery' to find information on mass extinctions, fossils and prehistoric life. http://park.org/Canada/Museum/hvpmdoor.html

☀ **Marine Conservaton Society** – UK charity working to protect seas, shores and marine wildlife. Other countries have similar marine conservation sites. This site has some great info and photos, and a 'Cool Seas' kids' site for younger children with some cool effects. Click on 'What We Do' then 'Education'. www.mcsuk.org

☀ **Met Office** – the UK meteorological office website, with facts and figures about climate change and the weather – click on 'Learning', then 'Education'. www.metoffice.gov.uk

My favourite's 'Wake Up, Freak Out'. What's yours?

☀ **Mongabay** – information, articles and photos on wildlife issues, and especially rainforests. The kids' site is at:
http://kids.mongabay.com

☀ **Planet Patrol** – a website on environment issues started by three young Australians, written by kids, for kids.
www.planetpatrol.info/main.html

☀ **Red List** – the worldwide list of threatened wildlife species as produced by the International Union for Conservation of Nature and Natural Resources (IUCN). The site is a little difficult to use, but the 'News' and 'Photos' sections contain lots of interesting info about specific species.
www.iucnredlist.org

☀ **TUNZA** – the UNEP (United Nations Environment Programme) website for Youth Action Around the World on environment issues.
http://www.unep.org/tunza

☀ **United Nations Cyberschoolbus** – website for young people, on human rights, poverty, and other issues including the UN's Millennium Development Goals.
http://cyberschoolbus.un.org

☀ **Wake Up, Freak Out – then Get a Grip** – a brilliant short animated film about climate change, watch it and pass it on.
http://wakeupfreakout.org

☀ **Water Aid** – an international charity helping the world's poorest people to get safe water and sanitation. The site has lots of information and facts about why people lack safe water, and ways you can help.
www.wateraid.org/international/learn_zone/default.asp

☀ **World Wildlife Fund for Nature** – a conservation organisation working for the protection of wildlife and habitats around the world and supporting the use of sustainable solutions.
www.worldwildlife.org

☀ **WRAP (Waste and Resources Action Programme)** – providing information to households and businesses to prevent waste, and encourage reuse and recycling.
www.wrap.org.uk

☀ **Young People's Trust for the Environment** – a UK charity working with young people on the understanding and awareness of environment issues. YPTE also provide school talks and courses.
www.ypte.org.uk

GLOSSARY

Words that appear in small capitals, LIKE THIS, have a separate entry of their own.

atmosphere   the layer of gases, including water vapour, and particles surrounding the Earth – also known as air. Almost all of the atmosphere lies within 30 km of the Earth's surface. Most of the world's weather happens in the lowest 6-16 km, known as the troposphere.

atom   a tiny unit of matter. Everything in the universe is made of atoms. Atoms contain a number of electrons whirling around a central nucleus, which is made of protons and neutrons. There are over 100 different types of atom, known as elements. Each element has its own symbol, such as C for CARBON, and O for OXYGEN. Atoms of different elements can join together to form different substances, such as CARBON DIOXIDE.

bacteria   microscopic life forms. There are millions of different types and they exist everywhere on Earth. Some cause infections and diseases, but many are vital for their ability to break down and change other matter.

battery   a container of chemicals that react together to produce a source of electricity when connected to a device.

biodegradable   anything that can be decomposed or broken down by microorganisms such as BACTERIA.

carbon   the chemical element C. Pure forms of carbon are diamond and graphite. Carbon ATOMS are found in all life forms and ORGANIC matter.

carbon dioxide   a gas with the symbol CO_2 consisting of two OXYGEN ATOMS bound to one CARBON atom. Carbon dioxide exists naturally in the ATMOSPHERE and the oceans and is produced by burning fossil fuels.

climate   weather patterns that happen in a particular region or area over a long period of time.

developed country   a term used to describe countries with well-established levels of business and industry, and where people generally have a high standard of living, including good education and health care.

developing country   a term used to describe countries with low or growing levels of business and industry, and where people generally have a lower standard of living, including poor education and health care.

Phew! So much information!

emission the production and release of something, especially gases, particles or energy, from a source.

erosion the process by which a material, especially rock and soil, is worn away and moved elsewhere by wind or water, usually in the form of rain, rivers, waves or ice.

extinct when no individuals of a SPECIES are left alive, that species becomes extinct and will never reappear. Extinction of a species can be brought about by the appearance of a new disease or predator, by another species competing for its resources, or by changes in its HABITAT.

famine a widespread lack of food in a region or area.

fertilizer a chemical or mixture of chemicals used to increase plant growth. Fertilizers may be ORGANIC, meaning they are made of decomposed plant or animal matter, or inorganic, meaning they are manufactured by chemical processes.

food chain the process by which energy is transferred from one living thing to another in the form of food.

habitat the type of surroundings or environment in which a particular group of animal or plant SPECIES will naturally thrive.

ice age a period of time when global temperatures are cold enough to substantially increase the ice sheets at the North and South Poles and form large ice sheets over land masses. Ice ages happen at various intervals which may be millions of years apart.

It takes roughly 365 days for the Earth to make one **orbit**, travelling at about 107,000 kmh.

orbit the path taken by one object or body as it travels around a particular point or another body in space. For example, the way a planet moves around a star. The Earth's orbit is like a squashed circle.

organic anything that is, or once was, living matter, or a part of living matter.

oxygen the chemical element O. Oxygen is produced naturally by plants, and is manufactured for industrial processes. Oxygen is vital to life on Earth.

pesticide any product that is used to kill or repel animal, plant, mould or fungi pests.

resource broadly, anything that can be used to support or maintain life. A resource may be natural, such as land, water and food; artificial, such as money or products; or include human abilities and skills.

species a group of living things made up of individuals that all share similar characteristics and can reproduce together.

sustainable something that can be used or worked in a way that will protect and maintain its future supply.

ECO-TIP... If it's safe to do so, clean up litter from beaches and riverbanks.

INDEX

G

gas, natural 15, 16, 20, 22, 28, 66;
genetic modification (GM) 58
geothermal power 33
Global Green New Deal 87
global warming 7, 10, 17, 22, 33, 35, 37, 84
Golden Rice 58
governments 11, 26, 60, 80, 82, 86, 88
greenhouse effect 12, 13, 22
greenhouse gases (GHGs) 13, 14, 16, 17, 18, 28, 35, 37, 86; see also 'emissions'
Green Revolution 83

H

habitats 10, 54, 76, 79, 80, 93
halocarbons 13, 17, 61, 62
HCFCs 17
health 46, 48, 58, 60, 63, 64
heating (buildings) 20, 21, 22, 30, 33, 48, 87
HFCs 17
housing 46, 47
hunger 48, 51, 52
hydrocarbons 35
hydroelectric power 31, 32, 33, 43
hydrogen 38

I

ice 10, 13, 79, 84
ice age 10, 93
incinerators 71
Industrial Revolution 14
industries 27, 28, 34, 35, 66, 86
insulation 25, 87
Intergovernmental Panel on Climate change (IPCC) 11, 83

J, K

jet fuel 34, 37
Kyoto Protocol 83

L

land 13, 49, 55, 61, 64
landfill 16, 55, 66, 70, 73, 75
land mines 53
land use, changes of 54, 79, 86
lead petrol 35
less developed countries – see 'developing countries'
life expectancy 46, 47
lightbulbs 25
logging 42

M

machines 14, 20, 23, 24, 47, 66
Marine Stewardship Council (MSC) 57
mass extinction 8, 10
matter, plant and animal 16, 20, 39, 77
meat 16, 43, 55, 58, 59
medicines 21, 40, 43, 46, 47, 48
mercury 22
methane 13, 16, 38, 54, 62; see also 'emissions'
mines and mining 43, 68

N

natural disasters 52
natural gas – see 'gas'
natural gas vehicles (NGVs) 38
neutrons 28, 92
nitrogen 13, 17, 22,
nitrous oxide 13, 17, 35, 39, 54
nuclear accidents 29
nuclear power 28, 29, 31, 33

O

oceans 10, 13, 14, 17, 56, 57, 61, 71, 92
oil 15, 20, 21, 22, 28, 34, 35, 66, 71
oil spills 83
orbit 10, 93
organic 22, 67, 73, 92, 93; farming 65, 87
oxygen (O) 13, 14, 17, 38, 77, 92, 93
ozone 13, 17, 41, 62; layer 17, 61, 83

P

packaging 25, 61, 63, 74
palaeontologists 9
palm oil 39
particles 35, 62, 63, 72, 92
pesticides 17, 46, 58, 63, 64, 65, 66, 67, 83, 93
pet foods 48
petrol 21, 34, 39
petroleum 34, 35, 38, 61, 62
photosynthesis 14, 41, 62
phytoplankton 14
plankton 61
plants 8, 10, 14, 35, 58, 60, 61, 62, 64, 67, 70, 77, 78, 80
plastics 17, 21, 25, 61, 63, 69, 71, 72
pollution 22, 35, 41, 60, 65, 68, 72, 76, 79, 82, 86; air 35, 37, 54, 60, 61, 63, 64, 67, 71; soil 54, 60, 66, 67, 72, 80; water 22, 53, 54, 57, 60, 61, 66, 67, 70, 72
polystyrene 61
population 46, 47, 48, 49, 51, 57, 60, 83, 86
poverty 50, 51
power stations 21, 33, 38, 43, 60, 62, 68

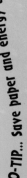

ECO-TIP... Save paper and energy and send e-cards.